Rolling with my Bosses

A Reverse Harem Romance

Rolling with my Bosses

A Reverse Harem Romance

Part of the
Eggplant County Roller Derby series

Sylvie Haas

SHhhh! I'm Reading...

Sylvie Haas

Super Hot Romance

www.SylvieHaas.com

Copyright

Cover design: Bookin' It Designs

Ebook ISBN: 978-1-950166-74-9

Paperback ISBN: 978-1-950166-75-6

Contents

Blurb

One way to get over my daddy issues... Find three new Daddies!

I can't let anything or anyone interfere with my plan to secretly work my way through the ranks of my dad's corporate empire.

Not even three coworkers who backed up some pretty sexy claims the day before I started my job. Small detail...I didn't tell them we're about to be coworkers or that my dad is the CEO.

I'm determined to prove that I can handle being successful at work while maintaining a fun personal life, namely roller derby, which my father despises.

Have I assigned myself too big of a task by adding 'fun times with three coworkers' to my to-do list? And am I the only one who left out a small detail about their identity?

If you love dirty-talking men who have over-the-top ideas of how to please their woman, you'll want to sneak to the mailroom with these coworkers, too!

There's a Prequel Short Story

If you haven't read the prequel for Rolling with my Bosses, you can grab it for free:

https://BookHip.com/BZNKNML

The link can also be found on my website:

https://SylvieHaas.com

Or you can jump right into the first day of Lexi's plan for her career...

One

Lexi

Today is the day I kick off my master plan. The first step in proving to my dad that success in business doesn't have to come at the expense of everything else...including family.

Sliding into the Human Resources office four minutes late, I'm not off to a good start. Driving to work in rush hour took longer than my trial run. Things to think about as I move back and start my life as an adult in this city.

I spent the last couple of years away with an aunt because I was problematic.

The buttoned-up HR lady looks over her glasses, makes a show of angling her head to the wall clock, then back at me with pursed lips.

"Did you understand your start time?"

"Yes ma'am. My apologies, I won't be late again." My brain is still mushy after yesterday's naughty fling, but I have to focus. The nameplate on the desk reminds me that her name is Monica.

I can't establish a reputation for slacking or disregarding the rules if I want to carry out my secret plan to climb through the ranks in my dad's company. With the last name of Smith, no one's going to realize who I am. Technically, he's my stepdad, but he's the only dad I've ever known, and adopted me before I understood what that meant.

Monica wastes no time ushering me to an office, sitting me at a computer, and explaining how the trainings work. She points me to the app I can download if I want to keep track for myself and have my own access to the content. Otherwise, I'm welcome to log on from a work computer.

My eyelids droop as I finish one monotonous video after another. I had no idea yesterday's orgasms could leave me so exhausted. That's not entirely true. It's the sleepless night spent thinking about three men who want to be my daddies that did me in. I couldn't get Austin, Bear, and John off my mind.

I'm not sure I should have messed around with future coworkers, but my friend Beatrix, who works here, commented about my V-card, in a way only a close friend can, then a few surprises had everything unraveling.

I laugh as an acronym comes on the screen—S.E.X. in large letters. I blink several times, thinking that my mind has detoured to yesterday. Nope, it's an acronym for the next video. I crack up, *Superior Ergonomic Xperience* is spelled out underneath it. That has to be intentional.

I had chuckled at the O.T.T., *Zero Trash Tolerance* acronym, and cursed my dirty mind for making anything of N.O.B, *Notification Of Benefits*. They're ordinary enough. But S.E.X. has to be intentional.

If only the training was as exciting as its name. And the next one, C.O.C.D., *Code Of Common Decency*. Perfect!

And that brings me to the S.H.I.T. training. *Sexual Harassment Isn't Tolerated.* No need to panic. Yesterday's romp was anything but harassment. And, yesterday, I wasn't an employee.

Yesterday...such a sweet memory. Three of my future coworkers gave me orgasms and promised to help with my V-card. I click 'Complete' and move to the next training video.

F.U.C.K.

My laugh is stifled by the meaning: *Fraternization is Unacceptable is Core Knowledge*

Crap. I didn't think rules like this existed anymore. I shift in my seat, tugging at the hem of my skirt as if it matters. I'm alone.

My heart pounds in my chest as I anticipate Beatrix jumping out and yelling, "Pranked!"

The cursor on the screen blinks. I remain alone in the silence. This is real. Anger bubbles up in me that she knew about the F.U.C.K. policy. That's why she cut me off from telling them I was going to be a coworker.

I hear about fraternization policies in movies but didn't think they really existed. Teachers at my high school dated each other, and I'm always hearing about workplace romances. Why am I presented with three spectacular daddies only to find out they're off-limits? Will Austin, Bear, and John be mad at me for deceiving them?

Suffering through the explanation that workplace relationships will not be tolerated, I click through to the next training. B.A.N.G.Z., *Badge Admittance and No-Go Zones.*

I want to kiss whoever made these acronyms—except that would violate the S.H.I.T. policy.

As instructed on the screen, I take a break to get my badge and test it. There's also a pop-up reminding me, as advised in the S.E.X. training, that I shouldn't be sitting for too long at one time.

Back in Monica's office, I sign for my badge, and get my list of admittance and no-go zones.

I'm dying to get to Beatrix to discuss her little trick yesterday. She knows I never would have let loose with those men if I'd known it was against policy. I have a wild side, but don't want to mess up my career plan.

On my way to her cubicle, everyone is heartily absorbed in their data entry, and many of the workers are wearing headphones.

I sit on Beatrix's desk, grab her earbud, then whisper-shout, "No fraternizing?"

"Deliver the mail, no one will care who you shag." She shrugs. "Everybody does it." She mentions a few names that don't mean anything to me.

I'm shocked. "Do you?"

She shakes her head. "But after listening to all of the wild water-cooler conversations, I went ahead with my cam-girl side gig. People are so horny."

"You should have told me about the F.U.C.K. policy. Or you should have at least let the guys know that I was going to start here today."

"You needed a nudge. Besides, what do you care about rules, you've come to my cubicle, distracting me from work." She taps my badge. "Have you been to the mail room yet?"

"Very funny." I told her that's where I hooked up with the guys. She'll hang that over me. "I'm headed there next to make sure my badge works."

"Ah, toodles." She wiggles her fingers and smiles huge. She's intolerable sometimes.

Two

Austin

Tapping my badge on the keypad, I wait for the light to turn green then swing the door to the mail room open. My chest deflates when the room is dark and empty.

I've reminded myself a thousand times that Lexi, my sweet Kitten wouldn't be here. Must have needed one more reminder.

The even harsher reality that I'm not ready to accept...our wild romp in the mail room might be the only time my brothers or I ever see her. She wouldn't give us her number, just said she'd find us.

My heart sinks. Did she rethink the twenty-year age difference?

My eyes stall on the space where John kneeled in front of her and ate her pussy. The cute kitten print on her skirt served as a hint of her innocence. Her orgasm was the most beautiful I've ever witnessed, and I'm tortured by the scent of her release lingering in the room.

John's and Bear's voices drift to me from down the hall, so I hold the door open. When we're safely inside, I click the lock. "You suppose she's going to reach out to find us today?"

Bear hangs his leather jacket in his locker. "I hope so, but I sure as fuck don't want her to think I'm a mail room clerk."

John looks confused. "What else would she think? We brought her in here to ravish her."

I point out, "But we never said we were mail room clerks." Only CEO Smith knows we're actually executives on a secret project.

Bear grumbles again. "I sure as fuck don't want her thinking I'm thirty-eight and all I've done with my life is sign on as a mail clerk for a major corporation."

Our apparent lack of success crossed my mind too. "This whole thing is fucked. Since when do we wait for women to contact us?"

"Since we haven't dated in years."

"Before that...when we dated, we made sure a woman knew we were interested."

"And we're all still single."

I ignore Bear's implication and focus on our connection to Lexi, her friend Beatrix who works in data entry. "Let me go talk to Beatrix, try to get Lexi's number. If we get in front of this, maybe she won't think to ask Beatrix what our job titles are."

John laughs. "They're young. They've already discussed us and scoured social media."

Bear smirks. "Which is another benefit of not being online."

Or a sign that we're dinosaurs compared to an eighteen-year-old. Are we senile for thinking she has interest in a relationship with the three of us? Will it freak her out that we don't have a public-facing record of every meal we've eaten and every good hair day?

Our avoidance of social media was a big factor in the CEO of Opus Syndicate putting us on this secret project to assess the employees in one of the corporations he swallowed up. Ironically, we're reporting on workplace ethics after bringing Lexi in here yesterday.

But I'd do it again. My only regret is that we didn't have sex. She wanted to, but everything was so new to her, it didn't seem right. And the only reason that's a regret is that she wouldn't give us her number. Said she'll find us. What if she doesn't?

Bear claps his hands together. "Get to work."

"I'll talk to Beatrix." I head out while they start sorting mail into slots so it can be organized into bins for efficient delivery.

Austin grabs a bin of mail and slams it into my chest. "You're heading down to data entry. Might as well get this shit delivered."

I was hoping to make a straight shot for her desk, but he's right.

Her cubicle is empty, so I step across the aisle and tap the guy on the shoulder. He turns, his eyes glazed over. I motion across the aisle. "Do you know where Beatrix is?"

"Why would I know?" He turns back to his computer. If he knew I was an executive for Opus Syndicate rather than a mail room guy, he wouldn't have done that. I'm forced to let it go. If anything, the CEO would be happy to hear his employee didn't waste time.

I step back across the aisle and reach for the pen cup on Beatrix's desk. The bright sticky notes and glitter pens remind me of the naughty notes I caught Lexi putting on her friend's Kanban planning board, and the note I wrote to myself without letting Lexi see.

How could I be so certain I'm going to marry a woman from the second I laid eyes on her? It blows my mind that a chance encounter allowed us to meet. But just as quickly as Lexi came into our lives and we gave her a few orgasms, she exited, leaving uncertainty.

I select a blue pen and grab a yellow sticky note, then write a message telling Beatrix to text me as soon as she's back at her desk.

I deliver the mail, and the second her text comes in, I rush through the sea of cubicles and make my way to hers. Not wanting to waste anyone's precious time I say, "We didn't get Lexi's phone number yesterday. Could you jot it down or send me her contact info?"

Beatrix squints. "If she wanted you to have it, wouldn't she have given it to you?" She has her friend's back, that's good, but really fucking irritating.

"You helped us hook up yesterday."

"I did." Her brevity scares the fuck out of me. Did Lexi not like...I can't accept the possibility. Her moans, her knees going weak, her bliss...she liked it.

"You're not going to give me her number?"

"No, sir. She'll reach out if she wants to get in touch." The smirk that Beatrix finally lets through tells me she knows Lexi will reach out, but damn. As I stand there trying to think of a way to convince her, she points for me to leave.

One point for the BFF with blue streaks in her hair. As much as I hate it, I'm glad she stood up to me.

Back in the mail room, I drag my hand over the counter where Lexi's ass had been. I say to my brothers, "We have another option. Her roller derby practice schedule and location are online."

"You don't think that would be stalkerish?" Bear asks.

A click from the door draws our attention. None of us have a single piece of mail in our hands as we talk to each other. Shit. It's Monica, the Human Resources rep assigned to this department.

"You gab worse than the high school gossip girls. If you don't get your work done, I'll write you up."

I grab a stack of envelopes.

"Don't test me. The new employee is going through the online trainings. She'll have her first day in the mail room tomorrow. Set a good example."

"We'll behave."

Monica points a finger. "I'm serious. She's young. A lot of potential. Do not run her off. And don't forget about the sexual harassment videos."

Bear scoffs, raising his hands. "Who do you think we are?"

"Interesting question given that men of your age who wear name brand suits, don't normally work in mail rooms. It didn't escape my attention that I was told to hire all three of you in one fell swoop."

I play off her accurate assessment. "Word has it CEO Smith fired the entire mail room, and you needed bodies pronto. We just wanted to be a part of Opus Syndicate. Lucky us."

She peers over her glasses. "Don't let your boys' club be a problem. You're not above the rules."

"Yes, ma'am." Bear nods as she turns to leave. "We don't want any trouble. We'll play nice with the new hire."

Monica pauses in the doorway. "I don't want you *playing* with her."

Three

Bear

"What are you doing?" Austin asks.

Sensing that his words are directed at me, I look at the envelope I'm sliding into the slot, check the name, and shift it to the correct place. I grab the next envelope.

"Hold on, Bear. I've watched you put the last five envelopes in the same spot. Check your work."

Exhaling hard, I throw my hands up. I don't know where I was putting anything. Scanning the slots, I notice one has decidedly more mail than the rest. Grabbing the lot, I sort the incorrectly placed mail and ignore Austin and John's grumbles.

I can't get my baby girl off my mind. With each piece of mail that passes through my hands, fear wells inside of me that Lexi has no intention of reaching out to us.

We'll have to work on Beatrix, or go the stalker route and show up at their roller derby practice.

Patience is not my friend. It's barely after ten. Why would I expect anything this early in the day? She probably has college classes or a job.

A click from the door doesn't faze me because a click means somebody has a badge. Probably just Monica coming in to see if we stopped gabbing as she put it. But when Austin's hand freezes midair I turn to see what's up.

It's Lexi. My cock twitches. Yesterday was casual sexy. Today it's business sexy. Her skirt is tighter, and her button-up blouse is more professional. Okay, work rather than college. But who let her in?

Her hands are behind her back. Does she realize that thrusts her boobs forward? A small purse with a long strap is slung crossways over her body, indenting her blouse along her cleavage. My palms itch to grab her tits. To grab her. To hold her against my body again. I don't understand how I can miss her this badly after one time, and we didn't even have sex.

"Baby Girl, you're back!" I can hardly believe it.

"What are you doing here?" She looks confused.

"We work here." I don't understand what's going on.

"In the mail room?"

"Wasn't that obvious yesterday?"

"I thought you brought me to the mail room because it was convenient."

"It was, because we work here."

"Did Beatrix put you up to this? People like me work in mail rooms. Not older men who wear expensive suits."

I remove a cuff link and roll one sleeve up then the other. "Does this help?"

Austin loosens his tie, and John tousles his hair.

"Beatrix had to put you up to this. The joke is over." Lexi doubles down.

"She didn't. I'm confused. Did she let you in?"

"No."

"Then how'd you get in?"

She slides a hand from behind her back and holds up a badge. "I officially start in the mail room tomorrow. Just doing my B.A.N.G.Z. zone testing."

Stepping closer, I verify that *Alexandra* Smith is indeed an employee. Her full name is too formal. Lexi is much more fitting. But more importantly, faking a badge would be more than Beatrix could pull off.

The amount of happiness exploding inside of me is incomprehensible. I'm ready to lock the door and pick up where we left off. I'll move double time on mail delivery if it means freeing up time to be with Baby Girl.

Lexi shifts nervously, worrying her lower lip.

My cock likes it when she worries, as long as she does that, but the rest of me isn't so happy. "What's wrong?"

"About yesterday...I didn't know about the fraternization policy."

John laughs. "You mean the F.U.C.K. policy? Rules are made to be broken."

I agree, but our jobs could be on the line. After all, our secret project is to report to the CEO about who's abusing the rules.

We devote all of our time to Opus Syndicate, long stretches of overtime. When are we supposed to meet women? Not that my brothers and I date, and we're not biological brothers. We served together and we're in the local motorcycle club. We'd die for each other. We do everything together and recently decided that the three of us combined could be enough to earn a woman's respect. To care for her the way she deserves. And yesterday we decided that woman was Lexi.

Fuck, fuck, fuck! This complicates things.

Lexi seems to consider John's disregard for rules, then says, "I need this job."

She needs a mail room job? I take her badge and loop the lanyard around her neck, freeing her hands. I close my hands around her, relishing how tiny they feel. "Baby Girl, do you need other things?"

I breathe deeply, hoping she'll give me the answer my body is craving. She pulls a hand free and lifts the badge that's hanging around my neck. "Bear is your actual name?"

I shrug then lean down for a kiss but stop myself an inch before her lips. "Baby Girl, I need you."

She rises on her tiptoes and pops a quick, chaste kiss on my lips. After all the lost sleep last night, every fucking dream I woke up from, having to rub one out, I'm full of energy and life and hope.

"I have to get back to my training," she says.

I grip her fingertips as she pulls away. "We can train you."

Austin steps behind her and wraps his arms around her. "And there's still a V-card we promised to help you with."

John has his phone out and is taking a picture. Did they plan this while I was focused on her? It's too smooth.

She pulls out of Austin's embrace and reaches for John's phone. "Did you take a picture?"

"Give me your number and I'll send it to you."

I'm not sure if she'll find that clever or creepy.

"If someone sees it, we can get in trouble."

"I don't plan on sharing it with anybody but the people in this room."

Lexi's expression says no, but she rattles off her phone number. "Nobody else."

"You have our word. But any time you forget how good we are together, I want you to check out your expression in that photo." John's usually the quiet one, but when he does speak, he has something worthy to say. Damn good idea.

Four

Lexi

My phone vibrates in my purse. I pull it out and look at the picture. Austin's arms are wrapped around me, the bulk of his body making a frame around mine. And my expression, John is right, there's no denying that I'm thinking, *Oh yes, Daddy. I want more of that.*

Oh no, my dad would fire me. I've never been so conflicted. I want to kill Beatrix right now.

Austin's voice pulls me from a million sordid thoughts. "We want our coworker to feel supported. Monica told us to be good role models. Didn't she, guys?"

John and Bear voice their agreement.

Austin guides me toward the mail bins, wraps his hand around mine, and in tandem we pick up a piece of mail. He reads the front of the manilla envelope, then drags it across the bay of mail slots.

"There's a lot to learn about how to slide into the right hole. I'd love to teach you." His hips roll against me, his thick erection taunting me. I'd laugh at his corny analogy if I didn't want to bend over and let him rid me of my virginity right here.

Bear picks up an envelope, and tugs at the loose corner of the flap. "I'm game to teach you about licking."

His tongue presses against the flap leaving me panting. I squeeze my thighs together.

And John, who has walked across the room and is at the door, says, "Sometimes we need to put our undivided attention on a matter." He flips the lock and walks back. "We have to make sure nobody breaks our focus."

My knees buckle, and Austin's arms tighten around me. It's enough of a jolt to pull me out of my swoon state. "We can't do this."

"Oh, Kitten, we can and we want to," Austin's deep voice and continued promises make me warm all over.

"We could all get fired. The CEO fired the whole mail room before...that's what Beatrix told me. The rumor is that they were goofing off and not getting the mail delivered."

"Then let's get the mail delivered so we can move on to coworker support." Austin assists me in placing another envelope.

"I want to...but..." Heavy breaths replace the end of my thought.

Austin says, "If the F.U.C.K. rule bothers you, we'll help you find a new job, or you can quit and let us take care of you."

"I have to work here," I say too quickly. Summoning every thought of my career plan, I slide sideways, freeing myself from Austin and his erection.

"Why?" He looks confused.

"I've had my eye on Opus Syndicate for years." That's true. "You switch to a different mail room." I'm still not convinced why men of their age and apparent affluence work here.

Bear says, "We've worked too—" He stumbles on his words, then regroups. "We've worked hard. We're up for promotion. Won't be in the mail room much longer." His chest inflates with the last statement.

I don't know what to do. I can't work somewhere else. My father prides his systems as being the best, so I have to show him that I can work my way up through *his systems* while not letting my work life be my entire life.

"Don't overthink it." Bear brushes my hair behind my shoulder.

John takes another picture. "You kill us with the way you gnaw on that lower lip."

"You shouldn't be taking pictures of me."

"Do you want me to delete it or send it to you?"

I can't meet his gaze. I can't believe I'm saying this. "Send it."

I need these. They'll help me round out my *have a life outside of the office* philosophy. Using these photos with my private sessions will be way better than using my imagination. And before I know it, Austin kneels in front of me. I pull fruitlessly at his shoulders.

"No fraternizing."

"I'm not fraternizing. I'm supporting my coworker." He wiggles his fingertips, which are gripped around the backs of my thighs, just below my ass. He nuzzles his face into the front of my skirt.

It feels so good, and I'd love a repeat of yesterday, but this can't be a habit.

"You guys need to stop dropping to your knees and..." The pressure of his mouth and the heat of his breath leave me at a loss for words.

He pulls away. "Need a reminder of where we left off? Inch your skirt up, and I'll do the rest."

The shutter-action sound from John's phone sends shivers through me.

"Send it." The throaty sound of my voice alerts me that I said that out loud. My fingers toy with the fabric of my skirt as bells go off.

It's my alarm for my next corporate-approved training session as opposed to these trainings. I thrust my hands against Austin's shoulders and am grateful when he gives me space.

"I have to get back. Monica will notice if I don't return." Flustered, I rush out. Should I trust Beatrix's assessment that the fraternization rule isn't enforced? Austin, Bear, and John aren't worried. Or should I give up my plan to work at my dad's company?

These guys are too good to be true.

Five

John

My brothers and I live together in a giant cabin. I heard them leave early this morning. We're all anxious for our first workday with Lexi.

When I let myself into the mail room ten minutes early, they're already there. We talked about Lexi and our desire to care for her. She's worth the risk.

Austin enjoys power positions and is willing to break a rule if he deems it unwarranted, such as the F.U.C.K fraternization rule that he deems micromanaging archaicism.

Bear likes to keep the peace and always has his eye on how situations can be smoothed out. He's convinced Lexi wants us to take care of her. We just have to convince her of that. His backup plan is that she's brand new and can work at a different company if it bothers her to break the rules.

In our own ways, we agree this thing with Lexi has to happen. Logistics will work out.

"How are we going to handle today?" Bear asks.

I look to Austin, who winks at me. “I liked John’s approach of texting her to wear a skirt that’s a little looser today and a button-up blouse.”

Austin stretches his neck. “As long as she doesn’t turn us into HR. I can’t get a read on her. It doesn’t make sense that she and Beatrix hid the fact that she was going to work here, and now, she’s worried about fraternization. Something’s not right. And why is she so attached to the Opus Syndicate mail room?”

“We all got to start somewhere.” Bear says.

“Which brings us to why she would want to hang out with old guys who work in a fucking mail room?” Austin slams his fist against the wall. I watch as he pulls his hand back, and I’m grateful the sheet rock isn’t damaged.

Bear goes for logic. “Let’s get this project done for the boss man and turn in our policy violators. So far we’ve got the extra-long shit breaks that dude in marketing takes and the frequent smoke breaks for the lady in procurement. We tried to drop hints and they didn’t take us seriously.”

“Yeah, because we’re fucking mail room clerks,” Austin can’t get over his irritation.

Bear has it mapped out. “We gave them a chance. They didn’t change their ways. We turn a couple people in and Smith lets us off this project. Then we’re back to our corner offices. We’ll have Lexi’s attention then.”

"Easier to convince her we can take care of her if we're her bosses than her mail room coworkers," I say as Lexi arrives in a loose skirt and button-up blouse as I'd requested.

"Your outfit's nice." And easy to fuck you in, but I presume that's understood.

"Thanks...umm...it's probably a mistake. I need *this* job at *this* company." She starts spouting about climbing the corporate ladder and that she's going to take classes, she just wants to get in the environment and be sure she's doing what's going to move the needle fastest.

I can't get my brain past the fact that this sweet thing shouldn't be working. She should be at home barefoot and pregnant, which is the exact opposite of what she says she wants. Good thing I'm prone to keeping my mouth shut. My thoughts are a personal and HR minefield, but I can't stop the thought of wanting to keep her full of babies.

As beautiful as she is, she'll be even more beautiful pregnant.

We should figure out a way for one of us to work from home any given day of the week, allowing us to physically be there for her. Babies can be a lot of work. My mind drifts off while she gives us a spiel that she clearly spent all night preparing. I force my attention back because this is important to her.

She wraps up. "So, I am going to work at Opus Syndicate and I need your help paying attention to the rules."

She needs our help...good, she's not convinced rules are that important.

My mouth gets ahead of me. "We've been slaves to corporate America all of our adult lives." I falter as I finish the sentence. Our big professional lives that led us to a mail room. We need to get back to our regular positions so we can be honest. I try to redirect the conversation. "I have no doubt, with your attitude, you can do whatever you want, but don't be a slave to the executives who only value you for your ability to make money for them. Make time for a life you enjoy."

Lexi's face lights up. "That's exactly my plan. I love roller derby and hope to get accepted onto the team here. I have a life outside of work, and I am going to continue that. You guys work in the mail room." She waves a hand toward the bins. "There are only so many pieces of mail and packages to deliver. What do you guys do for fun?"

I say, "You."

Lexi laughs, then tries to gather herself. "We aren't approved for overtime, so what do you do outside of work?"

"Hang out with friends." We can't afford to give up too much information, because we can't have her piecing together who we are, although I don't know how she'd do that.

"Okay." She sounds disappointed in my answer then gets a spark in her eye. "How long have you been working in the mail room for you to be up for a promotion? And please don't tell me that you started here ten years ago. That would kill my dreams."

"It's nothing like that," Bear says.

"So how long does it take to get a promotion from the mail room?"

"It's been...let me think..." Austin starts his answer several times, then finally says, "Long enough to know that if we don't get mail delivered, people are going to get grouchy and report us."

"And I won't hesitate to write you up," Monica's voice startles us. How did we miss the door unlocking.

"Nothing out of order here," Bear says.

A hint of relief graces Monica's expression.

"Wait." Austin steps closer to Monica. "Are you spot-checking us? Did you think we would be...misbehaving?"

Monica pushes her glasses up and clears her throat. "It's not like I go looking for trouble."

"But you're here..."

"I always check in with new hires. Make sure they know I'm here for them." I don't like the way she hints that we could be trouble for Lexi.

"Thank you, I do," Lexi says.

Austin's voice barely hides his tension. "Now, since there's nothing for you to see, we should get back to work."

He has no idea the genius statement he just made.

Six

Lexi

Clocking in, I say hello to coworkers who mostly just smile, nod, and mind their own business. Will a corporate career take that toll on me?

Is my father right that I'm not ready for this environment? Maybe, but not because I'm immature. I'm not ready to stop enjoying life.

A few days of work have proven to me that this is going to be harder than I thought. My soul is dead by the time I get off work each day. The drab office colors are a little more tolerable when I balance them with passing by Beatrix's cubicle to get doses of her bright colors and glitter.

Once I'm established, I'll have to funnel reports to HR concerning workplace morale. Colors other than beige and gray could lift spirits. And if we could make small changes, we might not have to get my dad's permission.

He doesn't approve of anything I love. He'd never approve of me hooking up with three guys at once.

Excellent. I made it a whole five minutes without thinking about the guys. When I get to the mail room, they're grinning. "Do I want to know why all three of you are grinning ear to ear?"

"John came up with a plan." Austin pauses and John nods for him to continue. "Monica can only write up incidents that happen in the workplace."

"Thank goodness, she won't be following me home."

"I'm being serious. She can only write up incidents that are documentable in the workplace."

"I get it. But I can't sneak around with you outside of here and—"

He holds a finger up then extends a hand and John puts a box on it. Austin pops the top open to reveal two bright pink items: a small remote control and a short vibrator. I'm almost as excited about the vibrant color as the items themselves.

"Giving me sex toys seems highly documentable."

"So you know what it is?" Bear is close on one side and John on the other.

I nod. "I don't want to get in trouble."

John says, "The other day, it dawned on me that you can't get written up unless the incident is documentable in the workplace. What do you say we have a little fun giving you orgasms without documentable touching?"

Saliva pools in my mouth and I swallow to avoid drooling. I love this idea way too much.

Bear says, "Let's call it a baby step. You're not ready for a relationship, and we can't deny what we want to do to you."

Austin pulls the vibrator out, drags it over my lips, and hands the box to John. "This could take care of that glazed-over look you get when this job bores you out of your mind."

"Is it that obvious?"

"Suck it."

I shift my eyes toward the door. John catches my concern and steps over to lock it. My tongue slides out tentatively as Austin eases the smooth silicone phallus into my mouth. I wish it was bigger. I wish it was real. I wish it was—I'm going to get myself fired.

It gently buzzes to life between my lips. Bear has the remote. "That's low. Want to find out what else it can do?"

With it still in my mouth, and my imagination running wild, I nod slightly. He taps the remote and my body tenses. I want more, but not in my mouth. It stops buzzing, leaving me breathless.

"Good Kitten." Austin pulls it out, takes my hand, and leads me to stand beside the table. "I can't wait to make you purr."

John takes my hands and presses them onto the table, "The door's locked. No one will see."

I worry my lower lip.

Bear hands the remote to John then grips a hand around my neck. Electricity shoots through me. The firm grip stirs up memories of the day before I started working here. The day I thought they were going to take my V-card. He'd held my throat tightly while John licked me to orgasm. The boys know what they're doing. And for some reason, they've chosen to do it with me.

Despite my efforts to be wary, I want to learn what they're so willing to teach—as long as it doesn't get too cozy. I can't fall for them. That's why I'm holding tight to my 'no going home with them' rule.

Keeping his grip, he lifts his pointer finger and angles my face to him. "Baby Girl, do you want to walk around with a fuck stick inside of you, while we take turns with the remote."

His hand constricts my answer into a garbled "yes".

He bends down, slanting his lips over mine, diving his tongue inside of me, and groaning as he pulls away. I'd pant if I could breathe better.

"Do you know how hard that makes me, Baby Girl?"

My head is feeling stuffy from his grip. I close my eyes and grin.

Cold air hits the backs of my thighs as someone raises my skirt. Austin kicks a foot between mine, prompting me to spread for him. I do.

I also question the very blurry line between considering this okay. It's turned into a game, and I want to play.

Austin rubs my ass cheek and tucks a finger into the lower edge of my panties. He slides lower until he's between my legs, scoots the fabric aside, and dips into my sex. "Naughty Kitten, you're already wet. Are you sure you don't want my long, thick cock instead of this little toy?"

I open my eyes and glance at Bear. He relaxes his grip on my neck, and I take a second to catch my breath. "You promised the toy."

"I promised my cock too."

"That was before I knew the rules."

He teases the silicone back and forth over the slit of my sex. "I'm going to have you begging for my cock, Kitten."

"I hope so." My mouth betrays me, but it must be the right thing to say because he slides the toy inside. I love the feel as the vibration starts. I meet John's gaze and gnaw on my lower lip to taunt him.

He rewards me with a sly smile and a few clicks higher.

Bear's hand warms my neck. I hate to say it. I'm sort of punishing myself because orgasming while he restricts my airflow is incredible, but I remind them of the agreement. "No touching."

"Baby Girl..."

My breath hitches as I push up from the table. "Back to work."

The first few steps I take toward the mail sorting slots are tentative, but I figure out the toy is secure. Doing my best to focus on departments and names rather than the toy, I perform my job.

The guys fall into place around me. Light conversation becomes harder to maintain. Then the tipping point threatens as my body is pushed to the brink of release. I crumble an envelope as I grab onto a slot divider and fall apart.

John steps beside me, turns the toy off, and swipes the ruined envelope from under my hand.

"I didn't realize just how much I was going to like not touching you."

Austin plucks the remote from his hands and my insides buzz to life again. He taps a button and the vibration pattern changes. "You hold all of the control, Kitten."

I appreciate his reminder. I could ask them to stop, or simply remove the toy, but I grab another stack of mail. They've found a way to help me forget about my drab, soul-deadening surroundings.

Seven

Austin

Another day at the office. Another day to be so close yet so far from Lexi. She sent a text explaining that she wasn't going to wear the toy today. She feels bad that it creates a one-sided relationship, but we're willing to wait for her to be ready for more.

In the meantime, we're inspired and we don't want her to think our relationship is all about sex.

I smile as Lexi watches John enter the mail room. Step one of our plan is unfolding.

"What's that?" she asks, staring at the book John is setting on a shelf in his locker.

"A book I checked out from the library."

"You check books out from the library?"

"Are you judging me?"

"Yes?" She extends a hand and we wait anxiously as he gives it to her.

"The History of Roller Derby?"

"I want to learn more about what interests you and reading is one of my hobbies." John generally reads on his phone, and not usually entire histories of sports.

"Oh, is it? Very cute. I won't ask to see a list of titles that you've read in the last month."

She winks at him and hands the book back. "Reading...that's cute."

"And helpful. The librarian didn't know we had a roller derby team. She's been fascinated by the sport but had a strict upbringing—no sports. We had a little conversation and I helped her look up the Hot Rollers. She said she's going to join. So if Belova Solonik shows up at practice..." He points at himself. "That's because of me."

Step two of our plan falls into place as we proceed to have a normal workday. When our first break comes around, I eagerly await step three.

We sit around the table and Bear angles his phone to her. "Which meal would you prefer? I'm taking cooking classes and haven't decided which avenue to pursue."

"You're taking cooking classes?" Lexi narrows her gaze then shifts it to John. "And you read?"

She sits back in her chair and crosses her arms. "I think you guys are up to something."

"You can bet your ass we're up to something." And we rarely fail to meet our goal, but I leave the last part off.

"Fine." Lexi helps Bear pick which meals to pursue in his class, clearly skeptical of his intentions.

As scheduled, we continue with normal mail sorting and delivering.

When I notice Lexi can't reach one of the top mail slots, I seize the chance to step close behind her. I pluck the envelope from her hand, read the name, and put it in the appropriate slot.

Here we go with my part of the plan. I brace my hands on either side of her then press my hips into her. "I learned that in roller derby, hip contact is permitted, but hands aren't."

"You read roller derby rules?" She angles her head over her shoulder.

"Like you said, I have to know the rules in case you want me to play."

"You mean to watch?"

"I like that, too." I love the way her laugh wiggles her body against mine.

"You're terrible."

"I like to know what I'm up against. I read that the jammer can give up her panty to another player. Have you ever done that?" I slide my hands along her arms, then shift one onto her belly, then lower it, sinking to her sex.

Her breaths grow heavy as she struggles to say, "You do realize the panty is a stretchy thing we wear over our helmets."

I rub circles around her sex. "Are you trying to avoid answering if you've ever passed your panty to someone else?"

Lexi nods. I don't know if she's avoiding answering or if she's passed her panty off, but I love that she can't think straight.

Then I pull my hand away. "Sorry, I forgot about the no-hands rule. I didn't see anything about teeth though."

I drop to my knees behind her, slide her skirt up, and damned if she isn't wearing panties with paw prints straight across the back.

"Oh, Kitten..."

Before she has a chance to say anything, I bite her ass. She gasps as I trail my teeth to catch the panties just enough that I can tug them down. Then an alarm goes off. She turns to look. I release her panties and they fall to her ankles.

"That's my alarm. I have to meet the delivery truck at the dock to get today's packages."

"I like the sound of you handling packages," I say as John opens her locker and silences the phone.

"You're supposed to be helping me follow the rules."

I grip her leg just below the knee with one hand and lift it to ease her foot out of her panties. Then I help her get her other foot out. I rub my hands up and down both legs and kiss her ass.

Bear takes advantage of me being occupied and grabs her panties from the floor.

"You boys." She turns around then extends her hand. "I need those."

"Not as much as I do." Bear laughs.

She huffs and pushes my forehead with one hand. I overreact, fall backward, and crash on the floor in front of her. I take a minute to admire her while she makes sure her skirt is back in place.

"Fine, we'll have it your way...I'll get the packages commando."

Bear's eyes go wide but she's out the door before he says, "That driver's a prick. I'll be back."

"Don't go running down there with that thing." I point at his erection. He adjusts himself, taking a moment to shift his pants and wiggle his hips while trying to get his cock under control.

Eight

Bear

I look into the hallway and she's already out of sight. The minute to myself could be useful while I wrap my brain around why I'm willing to break the rules with Lexi. Workplace rules are clearly spelled out and she made it even clearer that she doesn't plan on working elsewhere.

But being with her every day challenges me. There's no way I can avoid having a relationship with her just because we both work at Opus Syndicate.

At least I'm not a hypocrite. My brothers and I decided not to include anyone in our special project report whose only infraction is fraternizing.

How can I know in my soul that we'll convince Lexi to let us care for her? Is it just selfishness?

Now that I've got my erection tamed, I hustle down to help her in the loading dock. Before I get the door open, I hear a loud, irritated male voice. "I have schedules to adhere to."

Stepping onto the loading bay, my blood boils to discover the asshole delivery driver berating my baby girl.

Lexi's hands are pulled up in front of her. "I'm sorry, I won't be late again."

A sense of embarrassment washes over her face when she sees me.

According to my watch, she couldn't have been more than a couple minutes late. I appreciate promptness but even I know to chill over a fucking minute. I say, "She was ready to come down for the packages, but I caused a delay. Yell at me if you're going to flip out over a minute."

I detect a glimmer of excitement in her expression before she steels herself.

Stepping between them, shielding her, I square up with him and he doesn't back down. "If Opus would hold a tighter schedule, they might be able to retain workers. This mail room turns people over faster here than anywhere else."

"Don't ever talk to her like that again. Now help me get these unloaded then fuck off." I motion for Lexi to let me handle the packages, but she insists on helping. With both of us unloading, we probably made up for the damn minute.

Rolling the large bins into the building, creating distance between Baby Girl and the man who flared up my primal need to come to her defense, I wish there was a way to ensure she never had frustrations.

Her expression is pinched, forcing me to realize my heroics might not be welcome. Fuck.

It's not so terrible to want to help someone. What am I going to do, helicopter parent her as she climbs the corporate ladder. She'll never escape frustration. She'll probably end up getting into a power position where she'll work long, obsessive hours like everyone else. She'll give up roller derby and every other thing that she loves.

That was a quick downward spiral. I can't let that happen.

She pushes the UP button at the freight elevator. When we're inside, alone, she says, "Thank you for what you did out there, but I can fight my own battles. It's the only way I'll work my way up, so no more babying me."

Oh, Baby Girl, I want to baby you in so many ways. I keep the comment to myself. I do say, "The guy was a prick. I would've stepped in for anyone."

I'm conscious of the cameras in the elevator and don't want to give any security guy reason to file a report, so I keep my hands to myself. The willpower it takes to make that happen solidifies what's happening. I've fallen for her. I can't imagine a life without her. I'm going for it.

Her breaths are heavy and I can smell her arousal. "Besides, I think you liked it."

The freight elevator stops at each floor, but with us and two bins, there's no room for anyone else. It's a slow climb.

"Stop." Her tone is conflicted. "It's important that I'm respected for myself."

"I respect you, but I caught that smile when I protected you. Don't deny that it got you wet."

"Smiling doesn't mean I'm sexually aroused."

"No, but I can smell you, Baby Girl. And I know you don't have any panties on." I pull the wad of silky fabric from my pants pocket, bring it to my nose, and inhale. "You seem to get wet a lot around me."

"I am officially mortified."

"Owning that you're mortified...that's a power move. Not denying that you get wet around me...priceless. I'd fucking wear you like cologne if I wasn't worried it'd make every guy around me horny. What do you say we spend the afternoon shopping for new panties for you because I don't intend to give this pair back."

She extends a hand but I return the fabric to my pocket. She tries to grab them and I catch her wrist, wrapping my fingers around her delicate frame. Thoughts of pinning her against the wall, lifting her, even just inching her skirt up and sliding my hand between her legs awaken a side of me that's been dormant.

Remembering the cameras, I limit the rest of my actions to pinning her with my gaze and saying, "They're mine now..." I catch myself and clear my throat instead of scaring her off by saying, "You're mine."

"We can't just leave." She pulls away slowly.

"We can clock out."

"On my third day at Opus?" She raises an eyebrow, which is a fucking miracle compared to saying no.

I wait for the doors to open and close again, then offer, "We can say a bug ran through the mail room."

"What was it? The love bug?" She stifles her laughter and waves her hands frantically. "I didn't mean it like that."

"You're not too far from the truth. Come home with us. We're men of our word and said we would help you get rid of your V-card."

"Before any of us knew about our fraternization complication." She wants to do this. If I can just get her to admit it before our elevator cocoon thrusts us back to work.

"We'll figure it out. Just give us one shot each. If you're not impressed or insist on continuing working here, we'll drop it."

"Are you serious?"

"I am, especially when it comes to my intentions with you."

The elevator approaches our floor. She pauses, her knuckles blanching as she grips her bin. She's poised to bolt and avoid answering my question.

Gripping her bin, I hold it firmly in place.

The doors open. She tries to move forward but can't.

"Answer me, Baby Girl. Are we taking the afternoon off?"

"I'll get back to you."

Nine

Lexi

I avoid the guys the rest of the day. Without panties, I can't afford to get any more turned on. And I can't make up my mind. Everything up to this point in my life suddenly feels like a breeze. Two conflicting desires have never put me so at odds with myself.

I can't realistically expect three hot, older guys will ever again offer to show me how good sex can be. It's a carpe diem moment.

But getting fired from my job would ruin my career plan. The worst thing about all of this... I'm weighing one incredible sexual encounter against my entire future.

A huge roller-skating session to clear my mind in the park behind my house is in order. Any chance that can happen before my legs don't function anymore? A long hot bath will serve as a backup plan.

And whether I bring myself to clarity or not, I'll bring myself to orgasm with a long private session with the pictures John sent me.

My thoughts wander to Bear's earlier offer as I ride the elevator back to our floor. If I want to prove I can have a personal life and a successful business life, having a relationship is part of that. Relationship... I need to stop thinking that way.

This is heading the wrong direction. Going home with them would be a bigger wrong direction. Too intimate. We'd have to deal with the weird, *how long do I stay* thing, and I'm betting I'll be exhausted after the three of them. Plus, the less I know about them the better.

All I have left to do is return the mail cart and clock out. I can handle this.

Hesitating before opening the door to the mail room, I accept that I'll have to give Bear an answer. I whisper my pre-fab answer to practice, "I'm going to think about it tonight."

Encouraging myself to think about them even more is dangerous. Career-oriented Lexi steps in and points out that executives make hard decisions quickly. Should I practice that? Make a snap decision. No fear.

If I had to decide right now, my lady bits would win the vote.

My pulse races. Is there any way a spanking could be the only reprimand for the terrible decision I'm about to make? I swipe my badge. Turn the handle. Stiffen my spine. Swing the door open...and face a dark, empty room.

My body slumps. I have no idea if I'm relieved or bummed. I detect their lingering scent. I glance at the closed door.

No, Lexi. Do not masturbate in the workplace. Save that for at home...after roller skating and a bath. And probably dinner, but I don't think food is what I need anymore. I offer myself another piece of advice, don't call any of them Daddy like they encouraged when we met. That should help. My dad runs the company.

Exiting, I slide my badge across the clock-out station, and when I step into the parking garage, Bear is waiting.

"Did you spend the rest of the afternoon thinking about me?" His voice is low and slow, the way I imagine him talking to me in bed.

Why the hell did I look into his deep brown eyes? My nipples have joined my sex in casting a vote for shagging my coworkers.

My inability to speak gives him time to continue, "So you did."

"I thought about you, Daddy." Shit. So much for that gameplan. My entire body tingles. What happened to my pre-fab response about thinking? I need to get out of my head.

"Did you think about all three of us?"

I go for it. "All three of my daddies."

"So you're going home with us."

The intimacy of that lurches forward in my brain and a brilliant compromise drops into place. The votes are in. My body refuses to let me pass up their offer. "Going home with you is too much. But earlier, you said this could be a one-time thing."

"If you decide it's not worth continuing," Bear corrects me.

"If I call it off, you promise you'll let it go?"

"You're stinging our egos, but yes."

I close my eyes for a deep inhale and exhale. When I open them the guys are staring at me.

"You okay?" Austin asks.

I nod. "Is the mail room acceptable?"

It might as well have been rhetorical. The sexual tension is palpable as we make our way to the mail room. Until we're out of sight, there's too much risk to do anything.

Waiting for the elevator, Austin asks, "You have your toy with you?"

I pat my purse. "But this time I want the real thing."

He reaches to brush hair behind my ear but I pull away, not wanting the cameras in the parking garage to pick anything up.

"Give me the toy, Kitten."

"I don't want the toy, I want you, Daddy. All of you."

"You're going to have to trust me."

My insides melt. The thought of being able to trust someone so fully fills a void inside of me. He doesn't have unrealistic expectations or high bars. We're so naturally perfect together.

I pull the discreet box from my purse and hand it to him as we enter the elevator. A glance passes between the three of them. Bear and John stand side by side and Austin directs me behind them, placing himself beside me. The specificity of our positions strikes me as odd until Austin pulls the vibrator from the box, positions it carefully in his hand, and cups my ass.

My breathing hitches. Without panties in the way, this could be pretty easy.

Bear says, "Let him get you ready for your first time, Baby Girl. I've got the remote."

Austin whispers, "Spread your legs."

The doors start to close and my mind says 'wait until we're in the mail room' but my feet settle wider. My heart races.

He has to bend a little, and in a deft maneuver, the tip presses against my sex, which is so slick, he easily guides the toy inside of me.

"It's good," I say, as if he doesn't know that he's inserted it.

"I just like being inside of you. Go for it, Bear."

Vibrations light up my core. Austin's finger remains inside of me. This is far from the career path I laid out, but I've never felt so much like I'm heading the right direction.

"Fuck, Kitten. You're already tightening on me. What are you going to do to my cock?"

His cock. I've already seen that it's much thicker than his finger. What will that feel like? Bear kicks the vibrations up a notch and switches the pattern.

A few wiggles of Austin's finger, and control slips from my grasp. I grab handfuls of Bear and John's jackets, falling forward as my body winds tighter and tighter. The dings of each passing floor fade into the background.

I can't stop the rush. Bliss beckons me with its irresistible allure. I fall apart between my three guys, stifling my cries into Bear's back. I cling to them and pant for dear life that I can remain standing, I beg Bear to stop.

He takes mercy on me, Austin removes his finger, and the doors slide open.

"What's going on?" Monica asks.

Faster than I can process my panic, John says, "Lexi had a dizzy spell. We didn't want her to drive home if she wasn't well, so we're taking her back to the mail room to see if it passes."

"Do you need a doctor?" Monica is now inside the elevator with us, attempting to peer between Bear and John.

"I'll be fine, thanks."

Bear adds, "We have snacks and water. We'll take care of her. Get a doctor if she needs it."

Austin smooths the back of my skirt down. I keep my face buried in Bear's back. I can't be sure that my flushed, post-orgasmic expression will pass for the other kind of dizzy.

"Please keep me updated," Monica says.

"Will do." They shuffle me away from Monica, who remains in the elevator, and they flip the secondary lock once we're inside the mail room.

"We have to be more careful," I say.

"We offered to take you home."

"I might never leave."

"That's what we're hoping for," Bear says.

"One thing at a time." Plus, there's no bed here. No drifting off to sleep. I get to experience sex and no one gets tangled in emotions.

"You're always in control, Kitten. Tell us how you want it."

Bear's chest beckons to me as I recall the day we met. I leaned against his sturdy frame...

"Don't be afraid to tell us what you want, Baby Girl."

"Could we do it standing with you holding me like the day we met, but instead of a mouth, one of you has sex with me?" Will Bear remember the neck thing?

Bear takes my hand and pulls my chest against his. He says, "The only thing I don't like about that is that I won't be the first to slide my cock in you." But he doesn't hesitate to spin me and wrap his arms around my waist.

Austin steps forward, "Let me get rid of the toy so I can fill you with dick."

John lifts his phone. "Mind if I document this important moment?"

My nod is the go-ahead. Austin gets rid of the toy then unzips his pants. He's already hard. Mental assessments of his girth and the toy offer no comparison. I guess it's good his dick won't vibrate because that big and vibrating might kill me.

"I'm going to lift you. Wrap your legs around me if you want." Austin's hands slide behind my butt, curve down, and he hoists me against Bear. His rigid shaft presses hard against my sex, each little movement sending zings of excitement from my clit to every other part of my body.

If someone had explained this to me, I would have thought they were crazy, but sandwiched between these two men, I've never felt more secure or certain.

"Tell me to stop if you need a minute or if anything feels wrong."

I grip Bear's wrist with one hand and extend the other toward John, remembering their safety trick that I hold a set of keys and if I drop them, they stop immediately. Like a safe word but for when I can't talk. "Keys please, Daddy."

"You can just tell me to stop."

My tugs on Bear's wrist finally get him to relent. I guide his hand to my neck wanting him to lightly choke me like he did the first day we met and John gave me an orgasm. "Make me see stars."

"Baby Girl, this is your first time." His fingers resist my pressure.

"So make it good." I thrust my hand further toward John.

"Fuuuuck," All three of them seem to groan simultaneously.

"Take his cock before adding the choking."

I nod. John gives me his set of keys. Austin easily holds me with one arm, pulls the front of my skirt up, and stares between my legs at the wettest virgin pussy that's ever existed. At least that's what I'm assuming he's thinking. When he makes eye contact, I'm shocked at how that feels more vulnerable than the moment before. He moves in for a gentle kiss, then leans back and nestles his tip at my entrance.

My lower lips spread around his strained, shiny tip. The stretch burns but the hunger my entire body has for him wins out.

And I'm not the only one who feels the primal hunger. Austin's eyes and the clenching of his jaw as he starts pumping slowly, convey the same feral need. Bear tightens his grip. I glance at Austin, wanting to embed every bit of this memory in my mind.

The shutter sound of John's camera clicks as I glance his way. I can't wait to see the picture. I'm in control. I'm not conforming to anyone's rules but my own. And for the first time in my life, I'm good enough just because I'm being me.

Austin stretches me over the full length of his shaft, filling me, pleasing me, and making me wonder if a first time like this can ever be topped.

My orgasm builds exponentially as Bear increases pressure around my neck. The world disintegrates as our bodies mesh into one. Energy and euphoria swirl through me. The keys are clenched in my hand so hard, they're digging into the flesh of my palm. I'm caught in the whirlwind, dragged to the brink, and thrown over as my body tightens rhythmically around Austin's cock.

Stars explode behind my closed eyelids and air rushes back into my lungs as Austin relaxes his grip. Sensation floods me from everywhere. I'm crying out.

Each thrust of Austin's bare cock finds another crevice of my soul to ignite. He swells. I stretch. It's a dance governed by love.

No. I don't mean that.

His fingers dig into my ass as he roars his release, claiming me with every primal instinct. I've known at some level I wanted this. I want the most natural thing I've experienced my entire life.

My thoughts shatter as he climaxes inside of me. His warm seed filling, trickling, dripping.

I'm spent, but desperately want to experience sex with all of them. My clothes disappear at some point. Bear takes me against the wall, no hand on the neck since he wants me to keep my eyes open. Then John has me straddle his lap so he can enjoy my tits while he slides me over his shaft.

With the O.T.T. policy, there are no napkins or paper towels to clean up with. Austin pulls an extra shirt from his locker, slides it off the hangar, and hands it to me.

"After we all clean up, we can grab a mop from the janitorial closet." Bear winks at me. "Can't leave the floor wet. It might be slippery."

"I have some tissues in my purse. I can get it." I clean up and dress quickly.

"We'll get it," John says.

"It's not much. I'd prefer if you guys just go ahead and leave before me."

"Why?" Austin's tiny question is full of concern.

"I need a minute."

He wraps an arm around me, "You okay, Kitten?"

"I'm more than okay, Daddy. I'm going to let Monica know I'm fine then I'll head out." And I'm afraid that if I walk out with them, I'll get into their car instead of mine. With my insistence, they leave.

I slump into a chair and drop my face into my hands. I had no idea sex could feel like that. Not just physically but emotionally. They've unleashed a beast. I want them more than I want a career. I want the freedom they give me to be me. I don't have to prove myself.

I absolutely have to continue this with them.

But I'd be a fool to quit my job to do it. Which means I'm going to break the rules.

Ten

Bear

Rolling the sex toy remote in my fingers, I wish it could reach from the office to Lexi's house. I pull my hand out of my slacks pocket, letting the remote fall from my fingers.

Stopping at the mail room door, I'm at work an hour early. I couldn't sleep and figured my best chance of seeing Lexi was here.

I grab my lanyard and I'm about to pull it over my head when my phone buzzes. A message from HR. Monica needs me in her office as soon as possible. Could she possibly have found out what we did with Lexi? None of us would talk and Lexi would have no reason to unless her climb up the corporate ladder involved crushing men along the way. I don't get that vibe from her. She doesn't want to hurt anybody.

Lifting the lanyard from around my neck, I tap the badge on the keypad. Popping the door open, I confirm Lexi's not hear yet.

Letting the door close, I'll go straight to HR. Best to get that over with, but I pause mid-stride. I glanced at my suit jacket pocket and the neatly folded pair of new panties I'm using as a pocket square. I figured this would be a fun way to make up for all the panties we're going to steal or destroy.

Tucking one lacy edge into my pocket, I resume my trek to HR.

Rounding the door into the HR office, Monica is standing behind her desk, leaning forward, her fingertips poised on the top of the desk. Her lips are pursed, eyes narrowed.

"Is there a problem?"

"What are you up to, Bear?" She emphasizes my name.

I raise my hands defensively. "I'm an hour early. Is that suspicious to you? Are you watching the clock-in times?"

She leans back from her poised stance over the desk and crosses her arms. "What is it with the three of you? Something's up and if I figure out it's against company policy, I'll file every grievance possible."

"Just doing my job."

"Your job isn't to harass delivery drivers. And when I logged his complaint against you, the system triggered a pop-up to send you to the CEO. That's never happened before."

"The delivery driver filed a complaint? He's the one who was out of line."

"Normally, I would hear your side of the conflict, but I'm being overridden. I don't know what this is about, but I don't like my job being micromanaged."

I try to think of a defense for myself but she shushes me.

"From the moment I was told to hire the three of you, I've sensed something's amiss."

I can't tell her about the secret project, so I point toward the door. "Guess I better go see what Smith wants, so I can get back to work on time."

Monica confirms that I can leave. Smith's office is down the road a couple blocks, the building where I normally do my job as an executive for Opus Syndicate, which is why we aren't recognized in this building. Worry works its way through my body one inch at a time, digging into every nook and cranny.

Is what Monica said true, that this is tied to the loading dock confrontation, or a coincidence, and Smith knows we had sex at work?

Smith shows up at 6 am but doesn't schedule meetings before 8 am. I'm hopeful I can slip in without a wait.

His secretary makes one quick call to him and ushers me into his office. He's at his oversized desk with a wall of windows giving a view of the sunrise behind him.

He slides a paper with an image on it across his desk. My stomach knots. Cameras have gotten so small these days, there could be a camera in the mail room. There could be secret cameras everywhere. But no, it's the loading dock. I study the picture.

He motions for me to take a seat, which I do. My confidence is riding high with an easy explanation.

Smith says, "What were you doing with Alexandra Smith?"

I return my attention to the picture. "You mean Lexi?"

"Alexandra...my daughter."

His what? The paper falls over backward in my grasp. I'm studying his face. He's not joking. He never does.

Fuck! I tried to breed the boss's daughter. He'd be the worst father-in-law ever. No wonder Lexi has issues. No wonder she liked the idea of having three new daddies.

"She's your daughter?"

He nods and his eyes move down to my suit jacket. He points at my pocket square that's folded from panties that I bought for his daughter.

He says, "That pocket square doesn't quite match that tie and it's folded like..." He waves his hands as if he can't even think of a way to describe the atrocity.

True, the panties didn't fold into the proper shape, and the light blue isn't an exact match for my tie. No one but him would have cared.

"Never mind, just fix it."

I glance down and carefully pull the panties out of my pocket, balling them in my fist. "My apologies, I'll find a better use for this."

Smith narrows his eyes. I appreciate you taking this special project seriously, Garrett, but what was happening in that picture? You look ready to fight. I may have you in the mail room temporarily, but you must maintain professionalism."

I nod. A picture might be worth a thousand words. I was defending his daughter whom I just fucked. Not a detail I'm going to reveal.

He continues, "That extends to your dress. I don't approve of this sloppy presentation."

"Yes, sir." Fuck! I still can't process that Lexi is his daughter.

"Why didn't anyone tell me she was an employee?"

We didn't know she was your daughter."

"She didn't mention it?"

It's probably rhetorical, but I say, "No, sir."

He's having to think about that. "There's a motive, we just don't know what it is." He waves his fingers. "You can go. Don't say anything to her."

I take a slower pace back to our building. Do I tell John and Austin? Do we proceed with Lexi? Something doesn't add up.

Austin and John are sorting mail when I walk in.

"Where have you been slacker?" John keeps his attention on the envelopes.

"I'm five minutes early. That's hardly slacking."

"You left the house plenty early."

"I got called into HR." I scan the room for cameras, putting my earlier worry at ease. The bleak beige walls would make it hard to hide one.

They both stop and stare at me. Austin asks, "About Lexi?"

"The loading dock."

"We're good then?"

The door clicks and we all turn to watch Lexi enter. God, she's so fucking hot with that innocent, sexy vibe. She toys with her hair in one hand. I want to wrap my fingers around it and give a little tug as I angle her lips up to meet mine—preferably while my dick is inside of her.

Inside the boss's daughter. Jesus Christ this complicates things.

She smiles slyly. "Does anyone happen to know what happened to a little remote control I left here?"

John and Austin look around as if it's going to be laying somewhere. I shove my hand back in my pocket, not ready to say anything.

Austin says, "Keep that pussy ready for me. You don't need anything else in it."

"I just wanted to make sure that I knew who had it." Lexi puts her purse and coat in her locker.

"Do you have that little toy in right now?" Austin asks.

"Not until I locate the remote." She moves to the mail bins, looking in each one.

"Fair enough. Did you rethink the option that you could come home with us?"

"Hold on," I need to cut this off without sounding like a dick. "Don't rush her. She made it clear that she wants limits. Let her reveal her cards when she's ready. Let her show us her true self..."

I don't know what all I say. My brain is spinning out. The three of them are staring.

Lexi scrunches her lips. "Bear, stop!" She grabs her purse.

"Where are you going? You just got here," Austin says.

She holds up her badge. "I'm taking a break. I'll log it properly. But before I go, remind me how long you've worked here?"

"Fifteen year—" Austin stops abruptly.

"Days," John says. "We've been here around fifteen days."

"Yeah, just joking. It feels like fifteen years."

She leaves without looking back.

John slaps my arm. "What the hell?"

Austin joins him. "You act like you don't want her to go home with us. Don't confuse her."

John says, "Get yourself together before she comes back."

I have to tell them before she returns. "Think about it. Lexi Smith."

I pause "Alexandra Smith."

Austin says, "Okay, so Lexi is short for Alexandra. Big deal."

"You're focusing on the wrong part of the name."

"Smith?" John asks. "Isn't that the most common last name? His expression stiffens. "Although, you're starting to make me nervous."

"You should be nervous. We should all be nervous. Lexi is CEO Smith's daughter."

Austin and John look paralyzed as the information sinks in. Can't blame them. I'm still processing.

Austin says, "Does he know his daughter calls us Daddy?"

"We aren't fired?"

"I don't think he'd fire us. I think he'd destroy us."

I rub a hand over my face. "We can't care for her if we're fired. What I can't figure out is that she's the only one who knows all of the connections. What is she up to?"

They both look at me like I've lost my mind.

"She has to realize the repercussions."

Austin says, "But she doesn't know all of the connections. She thinks we work in the mail room. Not a hard job to replace."

"We can't tell her the truth, which doesn't leave us much room to confront her."

"A relationship like this is hard enough. Do we want it to work?"

Everyone agrees we do. I say, "Then we have to confront her. And we have to come clean that when we go back to our regular positions, we'll be her bosses. It's all about trust."

Eleven

Lexi

Making a quick stop at the time clock station, I log the start of my break.

When I step into Beatrix's cubicle, she's putting an earbud in. "Hey, take a break with me."

"Right now? What's wrong?"

"I need advice."

She logs the break in the employee portal then ditches her earbuds. "What's going on?"

We walk down the aisle between the cubicles and as we're getting toward the end near the stairwell, I whisper, "I've officially broken the company fraternization policy."

"You had sex with them."

"Keep your voice down." I throw the door to the stairwell open realizing the echo off the concrete is an even worse place to have the conversation.

She's thrilled but keeps her voice down. "How was it? Tell me everything."

"I'll tell you later." I lead the way to the roof. "What do you know about them?"

"You told me not to snoop."

"In general, as coworkers."

"They're new."

"How new?"

"A week or two? They're overqualified. They dress according to policy but at a price tag that doesn't match mail room pay. But you know that. Why ask now?"

"I was asking them about a...a toy they gave me, and I'm not elaborating, when Bear freaked out. Undeniably freaked out. It made me think about their elusiveness when employment comes up. The never give straight answers. Who stumbles on that? Did I make a mistake?"

"They're good guys, but you're right, something's not on the up and up. Let me do the snoopy-snoop. I'll see what I can dig up. I gotta protect my girl."

"I don't want you to get in trouble."

"I won't. Besides, my cam girl thing is stupidly successful. I'm going to quit this job soon."

"I'm so excited for you."

The fresh air on the roof calms me as we walk around the edge. The breeze tosses my hair, and I have to corral the wild strands with one hand, reminding me of the way Bear wrapped his fingers around it. I shake the thought. No more naughty plans until I know they're legit.

"Everybody has a paper trail. I'll tap into the records."

"You really should put your computer skills to work for good."

"This is good. I'm helping a friend."

"Thanks. This is so ridiculous. What am I going to do if it turns out they're just decent super-hot guys who have a thing for me? Should I quit? Give up my plan so we don't work together?"

"If they want to meet all of your needs, let them." Beatrix steps in front of me, grabs my shoulders, then points down the street. "But if it's important to you to work here, do it. Your father works in that building. He never comes over here. He's not going to find out. This is all he sees of us from his ivory tower."

I end up taking the rest of the day off so I won't have to confront the guys until I know more. Claiming the attention of three coworkers and having sex with them hardly fits with my goal of climbing to the top of the company unnoticed.

I'm grateful when it's time for a roller derby practice. Beatrix has information but insists she share it in person.

She's changing from her skirt and top into workout clothes when I arrive. She motions for me to hold on while she pulls a sports bra overhead. Already in my practice gear, I remove my outer layers of a jacket and sweatpants.

Beatrix cusses at the tight fabric, contorting to pull it into place while smashing her boobs. "Now that I'm making more money with my cam girl thing, I'm throwing all of these out and buying some with front closures."

My stepsister, Angel AKA Rolly Ghost, hobbles in with a brace on her ankle. It's a bummer that she's stepping back from the team as soon as I'm trying out. I wink since she's not injured. She hasn't revealed her pregnancy to our parents, so she's buying time. The problem is bigger than her pregnancy, though. She hooked up with my brothers, who are her stepbrothers. Our parents are going to freak. They wanted us to be a tight-knit family, not lovers.

Beatrix starts braiding her hair and meets my reflection in the mirror. "Do you want the bad news or the worst news?

Fear ripples through me. I take a deep breath. "Let's start with the bad."

"They haven't turned in all of their paperwork."

"They're already working. Monica was adamant all of my paperwork be completed."

"Yeah...and they don't appear to exist outside of their current positions."

Why is that a surprise? "You said they're new."

"They are, but the names on their employee contract don't exist anywhere." She weaves brown and blue strands of hair while I lace my skates. "I don't think the data in our system is real, Lexi."

"They have secret identities? That's crazy. They're just private. They live kind of remote." Serial killer vibes, anyone? I might have dodged a bullet not going home with them.

"People are private, sure. But Monica doesn't let paperwork slide."

I don't know what to do with that. "Wait, that was the bad news. How can it get worse?"

"I pulled the photos from their ID badges." She puts the rubber band in place around the second braid then reaches for her phone. "I did a reverse image search. These guys are practically ghosts."

"They mentioned a military past. Having shit to deal with." Making excuses for them feels right, although I'm sure it sounds weak.

"I'm all for privacy, but there's one picture." A wry smile hints on her lips. Appropriate for someone who just illegally snooped in personnel files. She turns her phone toward me. Bear is standing next to my dad who has his arm around him. That's enough to still my blood.

The brief caption below the picture identifies my father and Garrett Caylor—Bear's real name, at an elegant charity dinner.

When I questioned Bear's badge, he lied. Yeah, well...I'm going to give some grace with lying.

Garrett Caylor... Why does knowing his real name make my insides tingle? A desire to uncover more thunders through me. My brain, my heart, my sex. All of it is buzzing with the intrigue.

Garrett Caylor. Lexi Caylor. No, I shouldn't be doing that.

Garrett Caylor. Why does his badge list his name as Bear?

"You okay?" Beatrix has her skates on. Geez, how long did I get lost in thought? A whistle blows, letting us know it's time to get on the track.

"Thanks, Beatrix."

"What are you going to do? Remember, you can't say where you found out."

I push up from the bench. "I know. I should have known that fucking a coworker with the name of Bear was dangerous territory. Do you think my dad staged the whole thing so he could fire me?"

Twelve

John

The workday ended thirty minutes ago. Lexi still hasn't surfaced from this morning's break. And she's adhering to the P.I.S.S. policy, *Phone In Storage or Silenced.*

Does she know that we know that she's the CEO's daughter? Does she know that we've worked with her father a lot longer than our duty in the mail room? Too many unknowns.

I pull up her roller derby schedule.

Everything seemed fine until Bear freaked her out. His insistence that we give her space was overdone, but not completely out of line.

Did her dad get hold of her when she went on the break? Maybe he fired her.

She's going to have to face us and explain. Perhaps I'm being dramatic. Not talking to us for part of a day isn't exactly ghosting.

We wait outside of the arena where her team practices. Teammates file out. Some of the women notice us. Some look like they might be interested in our type. We've changed out of our work clothes and are sporting our jeans and leather jackets. Our motorcycles are twenty feet away, an easy connection that we're the ones who rode them.

Two women head our way but we motion them off. Beatrix is chatting with a friend when she comes out and we slip around the corner so she doesn't see us. No need to raise her curiosity. When she's gone, we wait closer to the door.

Lexi's car is still here.

Belova, the librarian, exits, sees us, and walks over. "Thank you so much for telling me about the Hot Rollers. This is going to be the absolute best."

"Glad you followed through," Austin says.

Bear asks, "Is Lexi still in there?"

"The coach asked her to stay for a minute. I think she made the cut to join the team. I've got to get back to studying."

"Thanks." I hate that we might dampen Lexi's exciting evening.

Belova continues to her car. There are only a couple of cars left when Lexi comes out. She stops in her tracks when she sees us, throws her duffel bag over her shoulder, and beelines for her car.

I rush over, stopping in front of her. "We need to talk. Come home with us."

She stops but looks at the ground. "Where is home?"

I figure it's an odd question, but what the heck? "We live just outside of Peach Bottom Valley in the Cherry Ridge foothills. Kind of in the mountains, near Eggplant Canyon, but we're in a more wooded area. We have a cabin."

"A cabin in the woods. That's a safe place to run off with three guys I don't even know."

Don't even know?

Bear caresses a hand over her shoulder, but she pulls away. "Sorry, I got weird earlier, that's why we need to talk. You're safe with us. You know that, Lexi. You know us."

"Do I? Garrett Caylor."

Silence traps us. She shouldn't know that. We wait for Bear to respond.

"Where did you hear that name?"

"Isn't it weird that we've had sex and me knowing your real name surprises you? Don't worry. I got the message loud and clear. We had a fling, it was fun, thank you."

"That's bullshit," Bear barks out.

She tries to walk away, but he grabs her arm.

"Let me go. You promised we could be coworkers and nothing more."

"That's not possible, Alexandra." She narrows her gaze at him.

"It has to be."

The arena door opens again and a woman with an ankle brace walks out, her slow pace turning to a run when she sees us. "Hey, let go of her."

She steps between Lexi and Bear.

"We're her...coworkers. We just want to talk." Thankfully, Bear defines our relationship cautiously. No need to rock the boat even more.

"I'm John." I calmly extend my hand. "And you are?"

Lexi pipes in, "She's my sister, but I guess we moved too fast to sort out all of our connections. You can quit your cooking classes and library trips. This thing between us was a blast, trust me, but it's over. I'll even return your little toy."

She waves over her shoulder as she storms to her car.

"That's yours to keep," Austin yells after her. "We don't have any other use for it."

"She's frazzled," her sister says. "She has a lot to process. She'll talk when she's ready, but please don't get in the way of her job."

Crap. Lexi thinks we're faking it with all of our newfound interests. Why can't she see that it's all because of her, and we're better people for it? She's shown us a different side to ourselves. All we've ever done is work.

How did she learn Bear's name? Maybe she's right. We don't deserve a woman like her.

Thirteen

Lexi

Adrenaline's a bitch. After the revelation about Bear, talking to my stepsister about her pregnancy, and getting accepted onto the Hot Rollers, I was all worked up and couldn't control my freaking mouth...blabbing Bear's real name. So much for using it as the element of surprise in a well-crafted plan.

With a web of deceit to untangle, sleep eludes me.

The next morning, I let myself into the mail room, prepared to have them demand an explanation. They aren't there.

Pulling the box with the remote-controlled toy from my purse, I set it in Bear's locker, which is never locked. No more play time until we clear the air.

I check the clock. I grab a stack of incoming mail and sort it into the slots. I check the clock again and grab a second handful of envelopes. Still no sign of the guys.

It would be nice if I could work without thinking about sex, but apparently, the F.U.C.K. policy is set with good reason.

How on earth can I work with these men after they've given me mind-blowing orgasms?

I have to get to the bottom of whether my dad's arm around Garrett's shoulders was a fleeting social thing, nothing more than crossing paths, or they actually know each other.

But something doesn't add up about their mail room clerk status. I can't entirely fault them for not being honest with me, because I haven't exactly told them who I am. But mail clerks don't get invited to thousand-dollar-a-plate charity dinners, and the date doesn't match their employment.

The click that precedes the door opening causes me to flinch.

"Grab your belongings," Monica's voice calls out.

I turn, surprised that it's Monica and not one or all of the guys.

"Come with me to my office."

"Is everything okay?"

"I'm going to decline to answer that."

That can't be good.

"Do you have anything in your locker?"

"A few..." I pause as my heart sinks.

She gives a sad smile. This can't be happening. Maybe it's a misunderstanding.

Once we're seated inside her office, she explains that I'm being let go and asks for my badge.

I grip my fingers around it. It's my pass key to the company. It's my pass key to my life plan. Ironic that I'm already attached to this symbol of belonging to a corporation when I harassed the guys about their dedication to it.

"Have I done something wrong?"

"You watched the F.F.S. training video, didn't you? You checked it off."

"Isn't it something about getting fired?"

"Correct, *Fired for Sanity*. It's a misleading name. Your first thirty days are a trial period, and if for any reason you're deemed not to be a good fit for the company or your position, you can be let go to save everyone's sanity."

"What can I do to fix this? Let me stay on a little bit longer." I'm shocked at how desperate I sound.

"I'm sorry Ms. Smith. This is effective immediately."

"Who determined I'm not a good fit for the company?"

"I can't say."

"Of course, everybody gets to hide behind privacy these days."

"Usually, but in this case, I simply don't have the information."

"Please double-check before firing me." I'm shameless in the wrong ways.

She closes her eyes for a moment before continuing. "I already double-checked."

My heart continues to sink. I would say there's only one person who'd want me fired, but I guess there's three. They had fun. Maybe had a thing for virgins. Or their egos got bruised that I wouldn't commit. Whatever. They don't respect me as an individual if they're going to get me fired for it.

Monica continues, "If it's any consolation, the records show no fault on your part."

"It's no consolation. This was personal."

Her head cocks to the side slightly. "Personal? How so?"

"It's not your problem." I hand my badge to her. I no longer have access to anything except the corridors and certain floors that the elevator allows public access to. I head to Beatrix's cubicle first, explain that I got fired, and she agrees that it seems like the guys are behind it.

"That's pretty fucking shitty," she says far too loudly. Again, not concerned at all about anyone in the cubicles around her.

She turns back to her computer and in a bunch of quick clicks and a little bit of typing, I realize she has her two-week notice pulled up.

"There." With a dramatic click, the form blips off the screen.

"Wait," I say too late. "No need for both of us to be broke. I might need a couch to sleep on."

She tosses her hair over her shoulder. "That cam girl thing is going gangbusters. Let's go to the diner, my treat. Cheri is bound to have something that you can drown your sorrows in."

"You're still on the clock."

"What are they going to do, fire me?" Her fearlessness is inspiring.

We ride the elevator down, and I imagine my stepsister having sex with my three brothers in a small space like this. I shiver. My path isn't so fortunate.

"You're going to be okay." Beatrix pats my arm.

"I guess it's good my dad didn't know I worked here. I'd never hear the end of it if I couldn't even stay employed in the corporate world for thirty days. He'd blame roller derby or friends with blue hair." I smile at her. "I thought the corporate ladder was going to be tricky to climb, but not for these reasons. I mean, one minute I'm having sex with three guys and Bear is defending me, and then they're getting me fired. I just can't understand guys."

Beatrix giggles.

I side-eye her. "That's hardly funny."

"No, but it gives me an idea. Our little outing to the diner is going to be a C.U.M. party. One last fun acronym for you."

"C.U.M.?"

"Can't Understand Men."

"Perfect! Can you come up with an acronym for my career plan being blown out of the water?"

Fourteen

Bear

Austin, John, and I stand side-by-side in front of Smith's desk, presumably not only for violating the F.U.C.K. policy but violating it while we violated his daughter.

The extent of my feelings for Baby Girl hit hard when I realize I'm more concerned with upsetting her than her father.

A text came in telling us to go straight to his office this morning. So, after waiting in the lobby for a couple of hours, here we are. It's interesting how the three of us can be standing in front of him while he sits in his oversized plush leather chair, and yet he dominates the room.

Poor Lexi. All I had been able to think earlier was what a terrible father-in-law he would make. She lived with this.

He starts spouting, "It's not easy running an empire. People hide their agendas from me. It's a good thing I can trust the three of you. I've considered how to deal with my daughter who failed to tell me she was working at my company. Again, personal agendas kept secret."

He doesn't know what we've done? Or is he saying that to see if we'll confess?

John is stoic but Austin shifts and clamps his fists together. Smith continues, "Alexandra thinks life is about fun and games. That mentality is risky in a serious corporate environment. She knew she didn't fit. That's why she went with secrecy. She's mischievous, but don't worry, I fired her."

I jerk backward. Austin says, "You what?"

"Family doesn't get special treatment. Everyone has to earn their place."

"Sir, respectfully, maybe that's why she didn't tell you. She didn't want anyone to think that she was using her name."

"If she didn't want to capitalize on her connection, why would she apply to one of my companies? Mischievous. She'll learn."

What hardened this man? And how did he raise a daughter like Lexi? The dynamic in their house must have been tense, and yet she's the most fun, light, and vibrant person I've ever met. Why would she sign on for more time with her father?

We may not deserve Lexi, but I can't stand him badmouthing her. My actions happen before I process that I'm ripping the lanyard off my neck, tossing it onto his desk, and blurting, "I quit."

I rush down the street and to the mail room where my hand reflexively reaches to my chest. There's no lanyard. On the off chance she's in the room and I could steal a moment with her, I bang on the door. "It's John. I just quit. I need to get my things."

No answer.

I lean against the wall, rub my hands over my face, and wonder what played out in Smith's office after I left. A few minutes pass before I hear my brothers coming down the hallway.

"That was dramatic," Austin says. John's shaking his head.

I rake my hands through my hair. "I can't fucking take him talking about her like that.

"We've got to sort things out with her," John says, as we enter the room.

"And how do we do that if she won't answer our calls or texts? We used our wild card tracking her down at roller derby. I'm sure her friends will protect her from us," Austin says.

Opening my locker to clear out my shit, my hand freezes midair. The box. Her gesture throws the weight of the world onto my shoulders. "Fuck. She's gone farther than not responding." I step back, prompting them to look inside.

"How about we put out a B.O.L.O. to our MC brothers?" John is already on a solution.

"Genius. With everyone on the lookout for her or her car, we'll find her."

"We should be able to crop one of our photos."

"Good plan. I can't let her walk away like this."

Fifteen

Lexi

Avery ushers Beatrix and me to the corner booth and stands at the edge of the table with her notepad resting on top of her baby belly. It's too big to call it a bump anymore. "Shouldn't you be at work? And happier? What's going on, Lexi?"

"Long story."

Beatrix says, "I'm treating her to a sugar coma."

"You want to see the dessert options?"

I shake my head and Beatrix answers for me. "Everything Cheri makes is wonderful. Pick for us."

"Will do. Anything else?"

"Can you serve up a job? I was let go." I shouldn't dump my problems on her.

"So sorry, honey." She's eight months pregnant, is on her feet all day in the diner, and doesn't have anyone to help her with the pregnancy or the baby afterward. And she's on hiatus from the Hot Rollers. She's sorry for me?

I self-consciously rub a hand over my belly. I could end up like her. How did I get so lost in everything that I had unprotected sex?

Avery's voice is light. "You can take my position. My last day is Friday."

"It's either that or let Beatrix teach me how to be a cam girl."

"She taught me."

"What?" I glance between the two of them.

Avery says, "I don't exactly have a savings account. Beatrix and I were joking around, and I tried the cam girl thing. That's why I won't be waitressing much longer."

"Cam girl? While you're pregnant?"

"I do foot fetish." She extends her neck forward, looking down. "It's getting harder, but I can keep doing it when the baby arrives. You'd be amazed what people will pay to see my feet. It's the most bizarre thing ever. But, hey, what do I care? When my feet ache at the end of the day, I can think about how much money they make me."

I'm captivated but the rumble of motorcycles draws all of our attentions. My heart's in my throat. I remind myself that Austin, Bear, and John are at work.

The bikers file inside. The first one is Mammoth. He's in the diner a lot. His eyes linger on Beatrix. Does he have a thing for her? She doesn't notice, but before I can say anything, Avery says, "Let me put an order in for you. Gotta take care of the regulars."

The bikers probably know my coworkers. Do they know Bear's name is Garrett Caylor?

Several minutes pass when the rumble of more motorcycles draws my attention to the parking lot. Oh, shit. It's them.

Avery catches the panicked look on my face as she's setting plates, napkins, and utensils on our table. "What's wrong, honey?"

"I don't want to talk to them." I make small motions with my head toward the parking lot as she angles herself in front of me.

"You can hide behind my belly."

That works oddly well, but I don't admit it. "I'm going to have to do this sooner or later."

Apparently sooner because Bear is peering over Avery's belly.

"Mind if we have some privacy?" he asks.

Avery waits for me to nod. "All right, Cheri will have your order out any minute."

With my arms folded on the table, I say, "We're no longer coworkers. Are you happy?"

Bear says, "We heard. Can we go somewhere to talk?"

"What do you mean you heard?"

"We heard that you were let go."

"Wait a minute." Beatrix slaps the table and I motion for her to hold off. "You didn't ask for me to be fired?"

"Why would we do that?"

I'm confused.

Austin tries to discreetly motion to Beatrix. "Do you want to discuss this in front of people?"

I reach out and pat her hand. "She's my support person."

"Then can we sit with you?" He motions for us to scoot into the corner.

I grab Beatrix's hand to keep her in place. "Say what you have to say and move on."

Beatrix says, "You're interrupting our C.U.M. party."

John cracks up. "Trying your hand at acronyms?"

I can't let them make this feel friendly. "You're focusing on the wrong thing."

Austin says, "No, we're finally focusing on the right thing. You."

Bear kneels on the floor next to our table. The sight of him taking a knee in front of me makes my heart flutter. Why can't I stop feeling things for them? For people who have deceived me? Besides, I'd have to backtrack my secret.

"I'm not much of a catch since I'm no longer employed either, but we want you. And two of us still have jobs." He motions to Austin and John.

Oh no, did he get fired because of me? Time to be a big girl and fess up.

"Roll that back. Before you talk about wanting me, I need to come clean. My dad is—"

He cuts me off. "We know who your dad is. Just found out. Why didn't you tell us?"

"I didn't want anyone to think I was using him to advance."

"Starting in the mail room?"

"I just graduated high school. I don't have a lot of skills."

"I beg to differ," Austin says.

I shoot him a look and he stops joking. "I just want to show my dad, or technically my stepdad, that it's possible to have a career and a home life. I grew up in his house, but he was hardly ever around. And my biological father left when I was too young to remember. I never felt important."

How about a side of daddy issues with that career goal?

Bear takes my hand. I let him. "You are important, Baby Girl." Austin and John move closer, voicing the same.

"He's so detached, I figured I could work at the company for years, if not decades, before he'd even know. And by that point, I'd be able to say I started five, ten, fifteen years ago, and prove to him that I was worth something and that I didn't have to give up a personal life to do it."

Bear squeezes my hand. "You're the most important thing that's happened to us, Lexi. Please let us show you that every day for the rest of your life."

This is dangerously close to a marriage proposal, which makes things even more confusing because I still don't understand whatever they're hiding. Then it hits me. I yank my hand away. "Are you using me for my connection to my dad?"

Austin speaks over Bear. "Exactly the opposite, Kitten. We love you despite your dad. He's a dick. We love you for having the balls to stand up to him. We love you because of who you are."

"Why risk being with me?"

Bear laughs. "I quit so there's not that much risk for me, other than if you'll have us, I'd see him at family gatherings."

"Whoa, slow down. We're not talking life plans yet."

"Well..." John smirks.

"But you two still work for him. He'd never respect you if you're with me."

Austin says, "We can handle that. For now, the two of us make more than enough to meet all of our needs. And we have savings because we didn't have a life outside of work until we met you."

Bear adds, "There are other jobs out there, Baby Girl. Your father doesn't get to control who we love and he doesn't get to control who we work for."

"He has a lot of contacts."

"Let's not get ahead of ourselves," John says.

Cheri emerges from the kitchen with what amounts to a giant glass bowl with layers of fruit, cream, and cake. "A Royal Cherry Trifle."

"It's huge. And it looks amazing."

"There's enough for everybody."

Bear grabs the edge of the table and stands. "I'm not sure if Lexi wants us to join her cum party."

I hold up a finger. "Shh. No jokes." But a smile breaks through my worry. "Cheri went a little crazy. There's plenty."

Mammoth steps to our table and I wonder if he's coming to see how big the dessert is, but he bumps John out of the way and taps Beatrix on the shoulder. "Looks like this booth is getting kind of full. Want to come sit at my table?"

Beatrix is wide-eyed, and I detect the excitement in her expression. I serve two portions of the trifle and scoot them toward Beatrix. "Go on. I need to talk to these guys."

Avery swings by with more dishes.

"I should wash up." I scoot out of the booth and stare at my reflection in the bathroom mirror. All my life I thought I had to prove something to my stepdad. I couldn't have been more wrong.

I don't need to prove anything to anybody, and it took three Daddies to teach me that.

The smile grinning back at me in the mirror is the widest, happiest smile I've had in a while, aside from when I'm having an orgasm maybe.

My first day working under my father's Opus Syndicate umbrella wasn't the first day of the rest of my life like I thought. I'll take the guys up on their offer to care for me. I'd be a fool to deny how much I'd love that.

It's a bold move, but I'm a badass woman in control of my life, and I'd much rather decorate their bachelor pad than try to convince a corporation to put color on their walls.

The bathroom door swings open and I focus on the faucet, turning the water on so I can actually wash my hands.

"Whatcha doin' in here, Baby Girl?"

I glance in the mirror. Bear's locking the door.

"Cleaning up so I can have dessert with my Daddies." I give a shy smile through the mirror.

He steps behind me and kisses the back of my head. "Does that mean you're finally gonna let us take you home?"

"I'm supposed to trust my daddies, right?"

I watch his reflection as he reaches into his jacket pocket. The discreet box is unmistakable. "We'll meet all of your needs."

"I have a lot of needs," I joke.

"Which probably explains why you need three Daddies."

He pulls the pink toy from the box, "And a few toys." He slips the toy between his teeth, drags it over my cheek, down my neck, and ends up kneeling in front of me.

"Didn't I tell you guys to quit doing that?"

"Must have forgot," he mumbles around the phallus. His hands run up and down the outsides of my legs then he slides a hand between them. "Want me to stop?"

"Never."

His grin is divinely wicked as he trails a finger over my sex and parts my pussy lips. He takes the toy from his mouth and slides it under my skirt, finding his way straight to my core.

"Now let's go have dessert." Bear turns the vibrator on low. I can't be sure, but I don't think I can hear it at this speed.

The minimal motion of the toy keeps me invigorated but doesn't consume me. How long could I stay in this aroused state?

We all settle in, eating the unbelievably delicious dessert. John says, "So, a C.U.M. party? You could work at Opus Syndicate creating acronyms."

"Beatrix gets credit for that one, Can't Understand Men. But the work acronyms... Whoever came up with those... How do they keep under my father's radar?"

Bear sets the remote on the table and the other two men smile.

"Do we need to leave?" Austin asks.

"I want to enjoy Cheri's masterpiece first." I motion to the trifle. "Tell me about the acronyms."

Austin feeds me a forkful of the creamy part of the dessert. John points at himself. "I made the acronyms. We're not supposed to tell you this, but we're not really mail room clerks, that's cover for a secret employee evaluation project Smith put us on. We're executives. We're actually your bosses in different aspects of the corporation. I'm in charge of staff development, Austin handles information technology which includes the mail room, and Bear oversees safety."

I nod and make a mental note to kiss John for his genius acronyms. The thought of them in trusted power positions with my father makes this even more delicious. My building orgasm ratchets up a notch.

"Like you said, your dad is so detached, he doesn't have a clue."

"So what exactly is your job?"

"I'm in charge of employee training. In a brainstorming session for revamping naming conventions for training sessions, I wrote Opus Syndicate on a dry-erase board then stepped back to think. I hadn't left a space between the two words, and the rest is history."

"Still not clear."

He drags a napkin in front of himself, then motions for Cheri to come over. "Can I use your pen?"

"Yeah, sure." She pulls it from her apron.

He writes then turns the napkin to me. I read the top line, Opus Syndicate, but underneath it, he spaced the letters differently: O-PUSSY-N-DIC-ATE

It's not perfect but I crack up. My hands fly over my full mouth. I swallow then say, "He'd die if he realized his fabulous Opus Syndicate is..." I just point.

"Exactly. I decided to make everything as ridiculous as the company name. He's so detached he doesn't even know."

"Wow, it's nice that someone else realizes it. I thought it was just me." I accept another forkful of cherries and cream.

Austin says, "Being detached from his business isn't his only problem. He's detached from the thing that matters most. His daughter."

Warmth and love flood through me, but it's not just Austin's endearing statement. I lost control of my restraint, or maybe Bear bumped the toy up a notch. I clench my mouth shut around my moans and try not to choke on the dessert. Not as fun as the normal choking I happen to like.

"That good?" Cheri walks past, smiling.

I nod and let my eyes fall shut.

"I love you, Baby Girl."

"I love you, Kitten."

"I love you, Lexi."

Their love carries me through another wave of orgasm.

Sixteen

Austin

Getting to be Kitten's Daddy along with my brothers makes my life purpose feel complete. The only way I can imagine it will get better will be when we get confirmation that she's pregnant. And of course, getting to be open about our relationship will be nice but that's a few steps down the line.

For now, Lexi asked us to keep it a secret since her stepsister and brothers, are about to reveal their relationship and pregnancy. And after clearing up our real names, Kitten said she didn't care because she's going to keep calling us all Daddy.

Otherwise, steps have fallen into place beautifully. Lexi quit her job and moved in, officially letting us take care of her. We wrapped up our secret project for CEO Smith, which allowed John and me to get back to our regular corner offices and roles within Opus Syndicate.

Bear took on the role of House Daddy, helping Lexi add colorful paint and matching furniture. While John and I are jealous of the extra time he gets to see Lexi during the day, we take pride in being the breadwinners and have negotiated work-from-home days.

And since we inadvertently made Monica's life miserable, we filled her in on the secret project.

Lexi's asleep on the new couch after a long night of making love that morphed into a morning of the same. As much as I want her to have the sleep that she deserves, my brothers and I are anxious to take the next big steps in our relationship, which are spelled out in the envelope I'm holding.

One of her legs has flopped over the edge, the other rests against the back cushion.

John says, "I've got this." He leans over the arm of the couch, inching under the blanket that's hiding Kitten's naked body.

We don't exactly have to watch where John's head stops to know what he has in mind. The sounds of his tongue lapping at her sex make my dick go rock hard.

A moan emanates from her as her mouth morphs into a smile. Her arms stretch overhead and her eyes flutter open. "I was just dreaming about this."

"All right, John, enough," I say and bat his head through the blanket.

"Don't make him stop, Daddy."

I flash the manilla envelope. "We have important business."

"Did you bring work home?" Her lower lip juts out and I want to throw the envelope aside, get my dick out, and rub it on her plump pout.

"You'll find out as soon as John gets out here."

She shoves on John's head and he retreats, rubbing a hand over his mouth as he stands beside us. "Miss Alexandra Smith, we have a proposal for you."

She sits up, trying to tuck the blanket around herself, but it falls below her tits and I'm focused on her rosy nipples that have taken on a deeper red and a little more weight than they used to have. I already know she's pregnant even though she said it's too soon to take a test.

I extend the envelope, which prompts her to give up fussing with the blanket. She slowly twirls the string to unwind it from the tab.

She extracts the paper and drops the envelope, which clearly has something else in it. The paper's too much of a shock though. John rushes to catch it.

"Marry Kitten," Lexi reads the rumpled, handwritten sticky note before pulling the bright purple paper off the page. She narrows her gaze at me. "I like the message, and the handwriting looks like yours, but since when do you use bright purple sticky notes?"

I kneel in front of her. "Remember the day we met?"

"Quite the first impression." She's bound to be remembering the orgasms we gave her.

"Do you remember me seeing your notes on Beatrix's Kanban board?"

A glimmer fills her eyes. "The ones I wrote about doing things to you and losing my virginity... Yes."

"And..." I wait for her to process a few more seconds of the memory.

"You grabbed one of her glitter pens to edit one of my notes."

"And I wrote this one."

She stares at the little paper. "You knew you were going to marry me?"

"I told you I was coming back for you. I meant it. But I can't steal the show. These guys want to marry you too." I motion toward the bigger piece of paper.

John did a fabulous job of coming up with an acronym for 'soulmate':

Speaking Of Us—Love, Marriage, And Trust Everlasting

Underneath the lengthy acronym, in a business memo format, is the request for her to marry us.

"Is this..." her words falter and her mouth hangs open. She reattaches the sticky note to the top of the page. Her chest makes distinct rises and falls.

John kneels beside me. "It's not my best work. That's a lot of letters to make an acronym but the offer is real. You are our soulmate, Lexi. Will you marry us?"

Bear joins us at her feet. "It's what all of us want. Your stepfather be damned. You're more important than any job we could ever have. You've shown us that life is about more than work. When we had that spark of an idea that between the three of us, we could do right by a woman, you not only showed us it was possible, but that we could do right by ourselves."

"Please marry us," John reiterates.

My heart races, I've never been more desperate for someone to answer a question. I know she'll say yes, but I have to hear the word from her lips.

"I will. I'll marry you. All of you. I love you so much."

We fall into a scramble of declarations of love and promises of eternity and happiness as we awkwardly hug.

"We have a couple of other things," John reminds us and we make space for him to hand the envelope back to Lexi.

She pulls out a photograph of Bear holding her against his chest, his hand around her neck, me between her legs, and she's looking straight at John and the camera. A hint of a blush colors her cheeks.

"You know when I took that?" John asks.

She raises an eyebrow. Lexi surprises us by saying, "I do. It was the day I became addicted to having a cock inside of me."

"There's that." John laughs. "It's also the day we got you pregnant."

She chuckles, "And how do you know I'm pregnant?"

"We're about to find out." He motions to the envelope.

She reaches in again and pulls out the pregnancy test stick. I feel the same way about this as I did about her agreeing to marry us, I need the confirmation. "Ready to make this official, Kitten.

She takes a heavy breath and flips the plastic test in her hands. "I've never taken one before. Do I just pee on it? What do I look for?"

John answers, "Uncap, pee on it, and wait five minutes. A plus means pregnant."

"And if it's not a plus."

"A minus means we keep trying."

"All right." She heads to the bathroom, her naked ass taunting us as she goes. I'm tempted to rip the test stick out of her hands and make love to her again. But I crave the certainty that we're a new kind of daddy. And I want to see her eyes light up when she finds out she's a mother.

When she returns, she sets the test stick on the end table and puts a tissue over it. "This is going to be five minutes of torture, and I want to be the one to read it, but could someone start a timer?"

"I already did. And we plan on helping you pass the time." John takes her hand and leads her back to the couch. "Now that our business is handled, we can pick up where we left off. Would it pass the time easier to see how many orgasms you can have in five minutes?"

"I'm primed. You left me hanging." She sits on the center cushion. John grabs her knees, parts them, and kisses his way up her thighs. She giggles and writhes, and I have to strip because my cock is about to rip out of my pants.

I love how happy Kitten gets. I move behind the couch where I can drag my fingers through her silky hair. Her nipples are tight beads. John switches his kisses to a lick. He flattens his tongue on her thigh, stopping to reach up and tweak a nipple. Fuck.

"I'll take picture duty," Bear says, and he snaps a couple photos. It's become our thing, one of us holding back, taking pictures. Her body shakes as John makes his way to her center, slurping, and I swear that fucker is being dramatic about it, but her body shivers.

I gather her hair in my hand, then angle her head up so I can lean down and kiss her. Her lips are soft and her gasps keep breaking our kiss.

"Come for him, Lexi."

"Do my daddies like watching each other?" she gets out between breaths.

"I like watching how you respond to him."

"Stroke yourself, Daddy."

"Fuck, Kitten." I tighten my grip on her hair, return my mouth to hers, and stroke myself. She can't see, but my moans against her mouth let her know.

Bear shrugs his clothes off, steps beside John, and fists his cock too.

I pull my lips from hers. "Look down at John while you come on his face, Kitten."

She glances at my fist pumping along my shaft and I move closer so she can lick the pre-cum, then I angle her head to John. He's looking up while going to town.

Her breaths grow erratic, her body twitches, and her hands move from gripping the blanket she's sitting on to his hair. Her hips buck and she tries to say something, but Bear catches my eye, grins, and steps closer to her, letting his pre-cum drip onto her thigh.

She falls apart, her sweet pleasure dragging me dangerously close to climax. I pause, step beside John, then let her watch me stroke while he draws a long full orgasm from her.

I steady my resolve so I don't blow my load yet. I want to be the first one to coat her with my seed when we find out she's pregnant.

John and Bear switch places and Bear opts to use his mouth. Maybe there's a thought lingering in each of our brains that if by some chance she's not pregnant, we'll have a load ready to go.

Lexi wraps her arm around my thigh. "I love learning how you stroke yourself, Daddy."

"It's nothing compared to having any part of you do it, Kitten."

She comes apart a second time, and I glance at the timer, confirming one minute left.

I prepare for the moment by easing her onto the floor, onto her knees, and lean her forward against the end table. "Keep an eye on that test stick."

I slide my cock into her, pumping slowly, waiting for the alarm. When John's phone finally buzzes, the need to release almost gets the best of me. I fortify myself. "Read it to us, Kitten. Give us the best news we've ever heard."

She lifts the edge of the tissue as I grip both of her hips, thrusting harder, my release imminent. Growls work their way through my chest, making me worry I won't hear her.

But over my groans and the wet sounds of my cock moving in and out of her, she adds the sweetest words, "Daddies, I'm pregnant."

I blow my load, coating her with my seed. Rope after rope of cum shoots from me. She's full, dripping, and I keep giving her more. My chest swells with pride that we've made her ours in the most intimate way. She's bound to us forever through the beauty of a child.

Epilogue

Lexi

Bear asks, "Can I get you anything else?"

"No, I'm stuffed." I sit back and rub my belly. There's hardly any room left for food, and I loved the spinach pinwheels he made for me for lunch. The cooking classes have paid off. He clears my plate, rinses it, and sticks it in the dishwasher.

Austin comes into the dining room and slides a smallish piece of paper across the table. I read it and laugh. He must have designed it on the computer, making it resemble a dollar bill, except that it contains a message: Good for one free FUCK

Underneath the message, he makes a decent acronym: Fill U with Cock, Kitten

"I've been watching the calendar. Today's the day the doctor cleared you to go into labor." He puts his hand on mine, which is still on the swell of my belly.

"I can't believe we could meet our little girl any day now." My heart is full of excitement and worry. The four of us aren't a traditional home, but what we lack there, we make up for in love. And we have the good fortune of lots of friends in similar relationships. Angel, Cheri, Beatrix, Avery...we're all hooked up with the guys' motorcycle club and live in Eggplant County, which has turned into the epicenter of ménage and reverse harem relationships.

Bear comes back from the kitchen. "Any day now. I've got the house in order, but man, I don't know how housewives do it. Living in the middle of the forest, a lot of dust gets in. I didn't care when it was just the three of us, but I've gotta take care of my Baby Girl."

He puts a hand on my shoulder and adds, "I'm gonna have to rethink that nickname since we're having a baby girl."

I don't want to give up my nickname, but don't know if we can make a distinction and use it privately. "I still like it for now. And since you've done such a great job keeping the house clean and have my bags by the door, I'm in the mood to redeem this coupon."

I wave Austin's paper in the air. Pregnancy hormones make me horny, and we've had to abstain.

"Sounds like a plan. Come with Daddy," Austin offers to help me up.

Before rising, I say, "I'm not looking forward to having to stop using that term. You three are the best daddies ever...my daddies."

"Don't go there. It's too painful," Austin says. "You'll always be Kitten to me. And I'm fine with you calling me Daddy if the little one's not around."

"Deal." I rise, with Austin and Bear's help, and just as I get to standing, I feel a pop. I'm pretty sure I hear it too. And wetness cascades down my legs. "Oh my god. Better grab a mop."

"Shit." Bear rushes to the cleaning closet.

John must have been nearby because he rushes in with dish towels. He throws a few on the floor and hands one to me. "Careful. The floor could be slippery."

Austin helps me to the side and steadies me while John helps me step out of my leggings. The amniotic fluid spreads like a freaking ocean over the tile floor. Everyone's helping clean the floor, clean me, get clean clothes for me.

It's surreal for the things we've read about and attended classes on to play out. Except for the intensity of the contractions. They're not light and exciting.

Bear is mopping next to me when pain grips my midsection. I grab Bear's shirt, doubling over with the contraction that seems to go on forever.

When it lets up, I catch my breath. "Is it supposed to hurt this much already?"

"Every labor is different," John reminds me. "But that contraction was over a minute long. We need to get you to the hospital."

"It feels like the baby's coming."

"Get her in the car, right now."

They bought an SUV so we have room to ride together. A necessary alternative to their motorcycles.

They rush me to the car and the second I'm in the back seat, another contraction hits. I grab the headrest in front of me.

Austin squeals the tires.

John's typing contraction times into one phone while talking to the doctor on another.

The rapid cycle repeats itself as Austin rushes us to the hospital.

"I feel like I need to push." I can't believe this is happening.

We all did Lamaze classes together, but I'm in the backseat with Bear since he was able to study more and practice with me as House Daddy. "Do you want me to check?"

"The doc says it could be time," John says.

"We're on the highway. Should I pull over?"

Bear says, "Keep driving. I've got everything under control back here." He eases me sideways and gets John to move his seat forward. Bear squeezes himself onto the floorboard, lifts my dress, and works my panties off.

"Holy fuck, this is amazing, she's crowning. Keep getting us closer to the hospital, and give me the towels from her bag." Bear demands. John hands them over the seat as the need to push builds again. He shucks a towel under my butt and says, "Go with it, Baby Girl. Push our baby out. I'm ready. Just do what your body tells you.

I bear down. The fiery stretch we read about consumes me.

Bear does a fabulous job narrating for all of us, saying the final, glorious words as newborn baby cries fill the car and all pain and pressure subside.

"I've got her. I've got our new precious baby girl."

John hands what looks to be one of my sweatshirts to Bear who's wrapping our newborn and handing her to me. "I can't decide which baby girl I love more."

And we live happily ever after!

Craving a little more sexy time with Lexi and her Daddies? A bonus scene is available by signing up for my newsletter. Once you subscribe, I'll keep you up to date on my stories, sales, and other Super Hot content you won't want to miss!

Visit my website:

https://SylvieHaas.com

And true to my initials, SHhhh, I'll let it be our little secret.

More from Sylvie Haas

Hang out in Eggplant County for Rolling with my Stepbrothers, Cheri's story

https://mybook.to/RollingStepbrothers

Or see where it all started in Eggplant Canyon!

https://mybook.to/EggplantCanyon

Sylvie Haas Freebies

Do you love bonus content?

Sign up for my newsletter and you'll get access to all of my freebies, and I'll keep you up to date on all of my new releases and special offers.

https://SylvieHaas.com

About the Author

Why Choose one hero when you deserve them all!

Sylvie Haas obsesses over dirty-talking heroes who fall hard and fast for the woman of their dreams.

On most days, you can find Sylvie with the wind in her hair, her fingers on the keyboard, and her mind in the gutter as she thinks up new places her characters can get frisky.

Sylvie Haas is the pen name of a USA Today Bestselling author who's been a finalist in multiple romance writing competitions and has been asked to present internationally on writing short stories and novellas.

Sylvie's books are short, age gap, ménage and reverse harem romances, that will satisfy you with a light and fun happily ever after!

www.ingramcontent.com/pod-product-compliance
Ingram Content Group UK Ltd.
Pitfield, Milton Keynes, MK11 3LW, UK
UKHW040849300326
11567UKWH00008B/29

9 781950 166756

Praise for *Women's Speaking Justified*

Margaret Fell's leadership, courage, and theological and organizational acumen were key to the success of the early Quaker movement. In *Women's Speaking Justified*, she not only responded to critics of women's public ministry but also set out a vision of how—from Genesis to Revelation—God works in history by empowering women and their voices. Fell is an "elder sister" whom today's female Christian leaders need as they pursue their vocations in the face of resurgent global patriarchy. Paul Anderson's new translation brings her insights to a contemporary audience.

—Rachel Muers
Professor and Chair of Divinity
University of Edinburgh

Anderson provides us with a much needed, approachable, and modern edition of Margaret Fell's *Women's Speaking Justified by Scripture*. The updated English is faithful and dynamic, and the introduction is excellent. It should introduce this important work to a new generation of readers. The original work by Margaret Fell gives a vibrant, energetic, and surprisingly detailed argument for the right of women to preach and teach in the church. There is a lot packed into this classic work on the subject; readers interested in women's studies, Quaker history, or gender in the Bible will find this a welcome volume.

—Sally Bruyneel
author of *Margaret Fell and the End of Time*

Margaret Fell's treatise on *Women's Speaking Justified* is as brilliant today as it was 360 years ago. She reads Scripture like an anthropologist, argues like a lawyer, and speaks like a prophet. Hearing her voice across the centuries, one recognizes again how deeply moving it is when the Spirit speaks through a woman.

—KAREN JO TORJESEN
author of *When Women Were Priests*

Margaret Fell's landmark work on behalf of women's ministry articulated this central Quaker principle more than three and a half centuries ago. Now Paul Anderson's graceful translation into modern English brings her classic work alive for the twenty-first century. His extraordinary work is most welcome and makes this valuable resource newly accessible for our own time.

—Stephen W. Angell
Leatherock Professor of Quaker Studies, Earlham School of Religion

The publication of this epoch-making treatise by Margaret Fell, now presented in modern English, comes at a singularly appropriate time, when we rejoice at the installation of the first woman to serve as Archbishop of Canterbury and thus as leader of the worldwide Anglican Communion. It also serves as a clear rebuttal to those who imagine that the struggle of women to be heard in the life of the church is of recent vintage and as a reminder to all of us that, no matter how staunchly we resist it, the power of the Holy Spirit will prevail.

—JUSTO GONZALEZ
author of *The Story of Christianity* (2 vols.)

Margaret Fell was among the major leaders of early Quakerism, and her defense of women in Christian leadership and ministry is clearly an important historical document. In this important project, Quaker New Testament scholar Paul Anderson has rendered this work into more accessible modern English and provides a helpful introduction so that Fell can be more widely read. Paul Anderson is surely correct that Margaret Fell deserves more serious attention.

—DANIEL SMITH-CHRISTOPHER
Distinguished Professor of Theological Studies
Loyola Marymount University, Los Angeles

Nearly four hundred years ago, Margaret Fell Fox offered a reasoned and scripturally based defense for women preaching and being called into ministry. Paul Anderson's translation of her *Women's Speaking Justified* into modern English not only ensures the easier accessibility of her text, but Anderson is also reminding us of the significance of Fell Fox as a theologian among all those who recognize the gifts and critical importance of women in ministry. Her essay should be required reading for all, men and women, engaged in Christian ministry and for those studying gender and the Christian faith.

—JACALYNN J. STUCKEY
dean, Division of Humanities, Education,
and Ministry at Malone University

Paul Anderson's translation of Margaret Fell's work makes it accessible to contemporary readers and contributes to ongoing discussions on women's ministry and biblical interpretation.

—ANNETTE POTGIETER
Senior Lecturer of New Testament and
Related Literature, University of Pretoria

Thanks to Professor Paul Anderson, we now have an inspiring new translation of Margaret Fell's powerful treatise, *Women's Speaking Justified*. Decades ahead of her time, here she embodies George Fox's encouragement to women, as well as to men, to speak that which is "inwardly from God."

—Elaine Pagels
Harrington Spear Paine Professor
of Religion, Princeton University

Rooted in Quaker theology and reverence for the Bible, Fell's work challenges silence imposed on women and affirms their spiritual equality. It remains a foundational and prophetic text on gender, authority, and Christian ministry.

—Esther Mombo
professor, Saint Paul's
University of Nairobi, Kenya

In *Women's Speaking Justified*, Margaret Fell articulates a pioneering and theologically robust defense of women's authority in Christian ministry, a voice that remains urgently relevant in the face of contemporary politics and renewed efforts to restrict women's gifts and participation in the church. Professor Paul Anderson's clear and disciplined modern English translation makes this foundational text freshly accessible, and it deserves close reading by scholars, church leaders, and all who care about Scripture, justice, and the public witness of Christianity.

—Dion A. Forster
Professor of Public Theology and
Ethics, Vrije Universiteit Amsterdam
president of the Global Network
for Public Theology

It is so important to have this key text readily accessible; Fell needs to be recognized as a key Quaker thinker and leader. Paul Anderson has done a fine job, too, putting the work in context.

—Ben Pink Dandelion
Woodbrooke Quaker Study Centre and
Honorary Professor of Quaker Studies
University of Birmingham

As one whose faith has been deeply formed by the preaching of godly and gifted Christian women, including many members of my own family, I am so thankful for the ministry of those like Margaret Fell who have answered the call to bear public witness to the gospel of our Lord Jesus Christ. As one who has been called to encourage, equip, and empower both women and men for the ministry of the gospel, I am deeply grateful for Paul Anderson's modern translation of this Quaker classic, making it even more accessible to a new generation of spiritual leaders within the body of Christ.

—David O. Williams
Professor of Practical Ministry
Malone University

In *Women's Speaking Justified*, Margaret Fell offered the world a robust defense of the Quaker conviction that, since the Holy Spirit had truly been poured upon all flesh, all people might now speak and act through its eternal power, regardless of gender, ethnicity, culture, or social status. Today, this remains a revolutionary message, and Paul Anderson has done us a great service in making Fell's text available to the modern reader in such an accessible form.

—Stuart Masters
author of *The Quaker Faith:*
Friends of Love and Truth

How strange that women's ministry is still a controversial issue in the twenty-first century! We need to hear again "the Mother of Quakerism"—Margaret Fell—on this subject. Thanks to Friend Paul Anderson for allowing her voice to be heard once again!

—Michael Willett Newheart
Interim Associate Dean of Academic Affairs
Howard University School of Divinity

Paul Anderson has offered us here a timely reminder of how complex and inclusive is the path from humans' "discovery" of Divine mystery, to the twenty-first-century re-discoveries, re-interpretations, re-visioning, and increasing re-understanding of the truth that none of us can flourish until—and unless—we fully grasp and recognize that the inhabitants of this world can flourish only to the degree that we recognize that care and respect and acknowledgement of the value of each of us is necessary for any of the inhabitants of this earth to flourish.

—Emma Lapsansky-Werner
Professor of History Emerita
Haverford College

Fell's work, written 360 years ago, is a foundational treatise in favor of women being granted a speaking role in the church. Arguing from Scripture that women are equally qualified for leadership, Fell's argument is still relevant to contemporary debates. Anderson's translation helpfully brings this work back to the fore, providing a needed historical perspective and voice to the discussion.

—Sean A. Adams
Professor of New Testament and
Ancient Culture, University of Glasgow

Margaret Fell's 1666/7 groundbreaking publication defending women's right to public ministry challenged entrenched patriarchal assumptions about gender and authority in seventeenth-century England. Long known mainly within Quaker circles, this historic and prophetic work now has a modern English edition that resonates with renewed power and relevance, ready to reach a much wider audience.

—Carole Spencer
author of *Holiness: The Soul of Quakerism*

St. Matthew describes the scribe trained for the Kingdom as someone who brings out of their treasures things new and things old; here, Professor Anderson plays the scribe, and in Margaret Fell's *Women's Speaking Justified, Proved and Allowed by the Scriptures*, he brings out a great treasure from of old. One might even go so far as to say that in the struggle for women's full participation in gospel ministry, this treatise is the pearl of great price.

—A K M Adam
lecturer at Oriel College, Oxford University
associate priest at St Helen's Church
The Parish of Abingdon-on-Thames

In this edition of Fell's pamphlet from 1666/7, Dr. Paul Anderson's translation masterfully preserves the original purpose of the language while adapting it into clearer, more approachable rendering for modern readers. Indeed, in this translation, a historical Quaker document that has endured for generations is now revitalized for future generations.

—Mark Condo
pastor of Reedwood Friends Church

Margaret Fell's contribution to the development of Christian thought has been underestimated outside Quaker circles. Her example and her writings sustained the witness of Quaker women who, generations later were the vanguard of the movements for women's emancipation in the church and wider society. Paul Anderson's clear and accurate modern rendering of her rigorously biblical justification of the right of women to speak allows her voice to be heard anew at a time when it is, sadly, still all too relevant.

—HUGH PYPER
Professor of Biblical Interpretation Emeritus
University of Sheffield

Anderson's translation renders Fell's message freshly sharpened. May her courageously prophetic word and life pierce our hearts and minds.

—CHUCK ORWILER
pastor of First Denver Friends, retired

It seems odd that we are at a point in our human and cultural journey that women in public ministry should even be an issue and particularly among Quakers, but here we are. It's because of this that Paul Anderson has done us a great service by preparing this special edition of Margaret Fell's *Women's Speaking Justified by Scripture* as an important reminder for Quakers and the larger church that women in public ministry should no longer be an issue but rather a holy calling that invites immediate and clear affirmation."

—SCOTT WAGONER
pastoral minister, High Point Friends Meeting
assistant clerk, Friends United Meeting

Margaret Fell Fox's *Women's Speaking Justified* is a thought-provoking, carefully reasoned defense of women's right to preach and exercise spiritual authority in the church. Written in the midst of the cultural and spiritual chaos of seventeenth-century England (1666/7), Fell reasons that the same Spirit of Christ who speaks through men also speaks through women. Most importantly, Fell provides a wonderfully reasoned and carefully nuanced articulation that the light of Christ, which enlivens every person, makes spiritual gifting and obedience to God the ultimate determinant of spiritual authority.

—Gayle D. Beebe
president of Westmont College

We are in debt to Paul Anderson for making available in an accessible form this seminal text, not just in Quaker but also in Christian thought.

—Thomas Hamm
Professor of History and Quaker
Scholar in Residence, Earlham College

Women's Speaking Justified by Scripture deserves to be published afresh, not only for its import in the history of Christianity but also for its verve and power. Margaret Fell's interpretations display arresting creativity and bravery worthy of scholarly consideration today. I'm thrilled to introduce this sister to my students so that they might know that the passion to allow God's daughters to use their gifts is not new but has always been championed by those who encounter God's word.

—Amy Peeler
Kenneth T. Wessner Professor
of New Testament, Wheaton College

Few of us have heard of Margaret Fell, who over three hundred years ago contributed the first thorough argument for women's public speaking in English. We should all be thankful that Paul Anderson has made her work accessible by providing a clear, contemporary rendering of her work and by offering a most helpful introduction. Fell anticipated many of the arguments still deployed against women's leadership, and her comments remain instructive, as is her witness.

—Greg Carey
associate dean for the Lancaster campus
and Professor of New Testament
Moravian University School of Theology

I welcome this fresh rendering into modern English of Margaret Fell's pioneering work on the role of women in Christian ministry. May it have a wide and influential hearing.

—Richard J. Foster
author of *Celebration of Discipline*
and *Streams of Living Water*

In *Women's Speaking Justified by Scripture*, Margaret Fell advances a social vision that was strikingly radical in the seventeenth century and remains contested today. The appearance of this new edition, translated into modern English and introduced by Paul Anderson, is especially welcome, reminding us that questions of who may interpret Scripture and speak with its authority are not merely historical but enduring and unresolved.

—Tommy Wasserman
Professor of Biblical Studies
Ansgar University College, Norway

Women's Speaking Justified by Scripture is an important, early attempt to explore the full range of biblical texts about women's roles as God's spokespersons and was composed by a woman while imprisoned for heeding biblical teaching. Margaret Fell, like the women who proclaimed, "He is risen," and "I have seen the Lord," did not deem her gender a reason to remain silent, setting also an example for women today.

—JUDITH GUNDRY
research scholar and adjunct professor
of New Testament at Yale University

Margaret Fell's *Women's Speaking Justified* is a courageous and faithful engagement with Scripture, written out of conviction and suffering. With clarity and reverence for the biblical witness, she challenges narrow readings that have silenced women, reminding the church that the gifts of the Spirit are not constrained by gender or by imposed structures of authority. This modern-English translation allows her testimony to speak with renewed strength and relevance in our time.

—KELLY KELLUM
General Secretary of
Friends United Meeting

This rendering of Margaret Fell's powerful pamphlet into modern English gives new life to a ground-breaking and erudite affirmation of women's public ministry. Enriched by an insightful introduction, Professor Anderson has made this work accessible to twenty-first-century churches, who will be challenged and encouraged anew by the biblically rooted arguments of this remarkable Quaker leader.

—SCOTT SPURLOCK
Professor of Scottish and Early Modern
Christianities at the University of Glasgow

Paul Anderson has done a great service in producing a contemporary English version of Margaret Fell's extraordinary pamphlet, Women's Speaking Justified, published in 1666/7. Margaret Fell, often described as "the Mother of Quakerism," and herself an effective speaker in Quaker meetings for worship, wrote this work while she was imprisoned for organizing faith services at her house. In a time when, distressingly, women's voices are still sometimes repressed in churches (under a misapprehension of two particular Biblical passages quoted for this purpose but taken out of context), reading Margaret Fell's justification of the importance of listening to all Spirit-led voices, including women's, is timely and refreshing.

—Laura Rediehs
Associate Professor of Philosophy Emerita
St. Lawrence University

Margaret Fell's

Women's Speaking Justified

in Modern English

translated and annotated
by Paul N. Anderson

BARCLAY PRESS
Newberg, OR 97132

Margaret Fell's "Women's Speaking Justified" in Modern English

Barclay Press, Inc.
Newberg, Oregon
www.barclaypress.com

Interior and cover design: Eric Muhr
Cover image: Thom Milkovic

ISBN 978-1-59498-211-8

Printed in the United States of America.

Biblical texts are crafted around the NRSV by Paul N. Anderson

This book is dedicated to my grandmother, Grace Coppock Clark, my mother, Lucy Clark Anderson, and my sister, Marva Anderson Hoopes—all recorded Quaker ministers—as well as my daughters, Sarah, Della, and Olivia, and my wife, Carla Cox Anderson.

Contents

Margaret Fell's Timely Treatise: A Foreword by Tim Gee

The decision of the Church of England to appoint the first ever female Archbishop of Canterbury is historic!

It is historic of course for Anglicans—and also for anyone who is a Christian in England—as she becomes the leader of the established church. It is also historic more widely, as she becomes one of the most high-profile female Christian leaders in the world.

Quakers haven't always gotten on with the established church. Despite that, this appointment is also important for us because, for many years, the Quakers were nearly alone in having both male and female leadership within their faith communities.

Nowadays, we are glad to no longer be alone, as most denominations have embraced greater gender equality, at least to some extent.

Still, though, there is a rumble of some people saying that "women's ministry isn't biblical." Some people even believe them and retreat from Christianity as a result.

That is a great shame. Republishing *Women's Speaking Justified* now is not a return to the war of words with other denominations that happened in past centuries.

Instead, it is a manifestation of rejoicing when the body of Christ rejoices. It is also an invitation, if you are a Christian brother or sister who is grieving this affirmation of women's ministry, to read *Women's Speaking Justified* in full and then to re-open your Bible and to read it once again afresh.

When Quakers heard the news of the appointment, some said, "At last!" while others asked, "I wonder what Margaret Fell would say?" Well, she isn't around anymore to ask. What we *can* do, though, is look at *what she actually did say* because, especially in its modern English translation, her words are as relevant now as ever.

—Tim Gee, General Secretary of the Friends World Committee for Consultation

Margaret Fell's Biblical Defense of Women's Public Ministries

Paul N. Anderson

Throughout the history of the Christian movement, roles of women in leadership have varied. In the early church, women were involved in leadership a good deal, although the public leadership of women was later somewhat replaced by men.[1] In the Gospel of John, women are portrayed in apostolic roles. The woman at the well becomes an apostle to the Samaritans in John 4; Mary Magdalene becomes an apostle to the Apostles in John 20. Indeed, she is the first to encounter Jesus following the Resurrection. And, the mother of Jesus presides over the beginning of his ministry at the wedding of Cana in John 2; she is also present at the cross in John 19. As Jesus entrusted Peter keys to the Kingdom after his confession in Matthew, Jesus entrusts his mother to the Beloved Disciple at the cross in John, a familial and relational image of church values and authority.[2]

1 See Karen Jo Torjesen, *When Women Were Priests: Women's Leadership in the Early Church and the Scandal of their Subordination in the Rise of Christianity* (New York: HarperCollins, 1993).

2 On the presentation of women and a Spirit-based ecclesiology in the Gospel of John, see Paul N. Anderson, *The Riddles of the Fourth Gospel: An Introduction to John* (Minneapolis: Fortress, 2011), 16-17, 221-235.

The Leadership of Women in Church History

While women are presented as accompanying Jesus and the Apostles in the Gospels, the second generation of the Jesus movement sees the emergence of house codes. In the letters of Peter and Paul, roles for men and women became somewhat defined, moving toward conventional structures of society and restricting somewhat women's roles in leadership. However, as believers in Greco-Roman society met in house-churches, women played important leadership roles in worship and service. In Romans 16, Paul sends greetings to a number of women in Christian leadership, including Junia, whom he numbers among the Apostles. There he also references Chloe as a leader of worship for those who gather in her house. Priscilla and her husband Aquila were teachers of Apollos in Ephesus (Acts 18). The Elder greets "the chosen lady and her children" in 2 John, sending greetings also from the chosen sister and her children—either a reference to another female church leader or a feminine reference to the church itself.

As the Jesus movement grew, however, moves toward institutionalization are clear. Whereas John the Baptist and Jesus challenged ritual purity and religious codes in the name of justice and authenticity, the movement developed its own organizational forms. Offices in churches developed as deacons, elders, and pastors. When table fellowship became unruly, Paul advised people to eat at home, moving from a full meal to a symbolic meal commemorating the Last Supper (1 Cor 11). Luke 22:20 shifted the *blood* of the covenant in Mark 14:24 to the cup of the covenant: a ritualizing move, tracking with Paul, there. Whereas sharing in the cup and baptism of Jesus in Mark 10:38-39 was associated with martyrological faithfulness, these practices later became reminders of the Christ Events and means of group inclusion (Matt 20:22; 28:19-20). And, following the death of Peter and the apostolic generation, Ignatius of Antioch called for the appointment of one bishop in every church, as a means of bringing about church unity within hierarchical structures. Apparently, the primacy-loving Diotrephes in 3 John 9-10 was one of these leaders, and John the Elder (the Presbyter) reports his inhospitality to "the church" (perhaps Antioch?), calling instead for those in his own community to show hospitality and to love one another as the basis for corporate unity (v. 11; 1 John 4:7-21; 2 John 1:5).[3]

Throughout the rest of church history, tensions between different forms of governance are numerous. In the second century CE, Spirit-led work of Montanus and his followers challenged institutionalism, claiming to be led by the Spirit in their worship and written work, and some of their ministers were women. Between Antioch and Rome, more hierarchical approaches to leadership developed, leading to the distinctive developments of the Orthodox and Catholic Churches (which separated in 1054 CE), although Spirit-led movements continued to develop in every generation and virtually every sector of the Christian movement.

With the availability of Scripture precipitating the Reformation in the 16th century and following, Protestants and others pulled away from some of the hierarchical structures of the established churches.

---

3 John the Presbyter then finalized the witness of the Beloved Disciple after his death (John 21:20-24), as a corrective to rising institutionalism at the end of the first century CE, arguing for a more primitive familial, egalitarian, and Spirit-based view of church leadership rooted in historical memory, over and against emerging trends (Anderson, *Riddles*, 221-235). See also Paul N. Anderson, "Was the Fourth Evangelist a Quaker?" *Quaker Religious Thought* 76 (1991): 37-43.

This included the Quaker movement in England a century or so later, as part of the Puritan movement, seeking to embody "primitive Christianity revived."[4] However, while the Reformers made good headway in discerning the receiving of God's grace by faith as the heart of the gospel, they tended to build doctrines based upon what George Fox described as "chapter-and-verse" proof-texts. Thus, in addition to the established churches, they also viewed Paul's forbidding of women to speak in worship in legalistic terms, rather than considering the contextual backdrop of biblical texts involved. And, this is where the contributions of George Fox and Margaret Fell came into play.

Margaret Fell's *Women's Speaking Justified by Scripture*

While George Fox is considered the founder of the Quaker movement—the Religious Society of Friends (John 15:12-15)—Margaret Fell is also rightly seen as "the Mother of Quakerism."[5] Margaret Askew (1614-1702) was married to Thomas Fell (1598-1658) in 1632, and Thomas became judge of assize for the Chester and North Wales circuit. He was also a member of Parliament, so the couple had great influence in

4 This was William Penn's (correct, I believe) assessment of the central vision of the Quaker movement. Paul N. Anderson, "'Primitive Christianity Revived'—The Original Quaker Vision," *Quaker Religious Thought* 131 (2018): 5-24.

5 Isabel Ross, *Margaret Fell: Mother of Quakerism* (2nd edn. Sessions: York, 1984). See also Bonnelyn Young Kunze, *Margaret Fell and the Rise of Quakerism* (Stanford: Stanford University Press, 1994); ed. Elsa F. Glines, *Undaunted Zeal: The Letters of Margaret Fell* (Richmond, IN; Friends United Press, 2003); Sally Bruyneel, *Margaret Fell and the End of Time: The Theology of the Mother of Quakerism* (Waco, TX: Baylor University Press, 2010).

Northwest England during and after the English Civil War(s) (1642-1651). It should also be noted that without their protection and support, the Quaker movement would by no means have enjoyed such a vibrant and explosive beginning. When George Fox visited and spoke in their church in Ulverston in June of 1652, his words were life-changing for Margaret. Rather than seeing Christian faith as a set of fixed doctrines or biblical tenets constructed by others, her life was transformed by the probing query of George Fox: "...what canst thou say..., and what thou speakest, is it inwardly from God?"

This conviction, that authentic faith and practice should originate from first-hand encounter with the Divine, changed her life, and Margaret became a lifelong proponent of this life-changing gospel message. Over the next half-century, Swarthmoor Hall—the Fell home—became the central headquarters of the early Quaker movement. Margaret also helped organize the Kendal Fund, which supported Friends traveling ministries and organized the care of imprisoned Friends throughout the land. Because of her connection to English royalty and national leadership, she carried the 1660 letter of a dozen Quaker leaders to King Charles II, marking the first declaration of the Quaker Peace Testimony.[6]

6 In my analysis of the historic Quaker Peace Testimony document, no fewer than forty additional biblical texts can be found within the document, alluded to indirectly, in addition to the handful of texts referenced explicitly. Thus, this momentous document reflects biblical convictions at the heart of the social conscience of early Quaker leaders. Paul N. Anderson, "Introduction and Acknowledgments," *Quakers and the Future of Peacemaking*, Quakers and the Disciplines 8, Alonzo Valentine, Paul N. Anderson, and Christy Randazzo, eds. (FAHE Longmeadow, MA: Full Media Services, 2024), 1-11.

Eleven years after the passing of her first husband (1658), Margaret married George Fox, and the two of them—the dynamic duo of Quaker leadership—partnered together in furthering the Friends movement. George conducted extensive travels around Britain and to the Americas, and Margaret developed and established separate meetings for Quaker women, allowing their voices to be expressed and heard, unencumbered by male influence. As they both suffered a number of further imprisonments, the time they were able to spend together before George's death in 1691 was minimal, perhaps amounting to only a couple of years overall. Nonetheless, Margaret supported the larger movement extensively with her letters and writings, and she and her daughters Isabel and Sarah contributed valuably to the advance and progress of the Quaker movement.

Among Margaret's two dozen or so writings, her most significant was written during her Lancaster Castle imprisonment (1664-1668), where she addressed critically and creatively the standard exclusion of women's preaching, based on surface-readings of particular biblical passages. She had been imprisoned for holding worship in her home, against the Conventicle Act, one of four anti-Quaker laws instituted by the English government between 1661 and 1665. Margaret Hope Bacon claimed that this publication was the first post-Reformation book written by a woman, and it certainly is the first full-length treatment of the subject in English or otherwise.[7] In a briefer though more strident way, Marie Dentière wrote *A Very Useful Epistle* in French (1539), opening the door to the subject of women in Christian leadership. In addition to defending John Calvin and the Reformers in Geneva, she argued for the

---

7 Margaret Hope Bacon, *Mothers of Feminism* (New York: Harper & Row, 1986), 16.

capacity of women to study and learn and thus to teach Christian theology and the contents of Scripture.[8] In addition, persecuted leading women in the fifteenth through the seventeenth centuries often testified faithfully to their sense of spiritual calling, but Fell's treatise is the first fully argued exegetical defense of women in ministry in modern times.[9]

George Fox had also challenged the issue of women's subservience to their husbands in 1656,[10] arguing that women prophesying at Pentecost (Acts 2) fulfilled the Prophecy of Joel 2:28-32, as an eschatological manifestation of the Holy Spirit. Further, Fox notes a number of biblical cases where women are presented as carrying forth public ministry, fulfilling the yearning of Moses that all God's people would be prophets, and that he would pour forth his Spirit on all of them (Num 11:29). As Anna prophesied in the temple (Luke 2), as Paul ministered alongside women in his ministry (Romans 16), as Priscilla and Aquila instructed Apollos (Acts 18), and as Paul referenced ministering women in his writing (Phil 4), Fox championed the counsel of Paul in 1 Thessalonians 5:19-20—"Do not quench the Spirit. Do not despise prophecies."—applying the text to women's ministries in particular (*Epistles* 283).

8 Marie Dentière, *Epistle to Marguerite de Navarre and Preface to a Sermon by John Calvin,* edited and translated by Mary B. McKinley (Chicago: University of Chicago Press, 2004). Later, Calvin included her comments in his 1561 sermon on 1 Timothy 2, regarding the modesty and demeanor of women's actions as the issue, rather than the substance of their teachings.

9 See, for instance, Genelle Gertz (ed.), *Heresy Trials of English Women Writers, 1400-1670* (Cambridge: Cambridge University Press, 2012).

10 George Fox, "The Woman Learning in Silence, Or the Mystery of the Woman's Subjection to her Husband," *The Works of George Fox, Vol. 4, The Doctrinals, Vol. 1* (1831, State College, PA: New Foundation, 1990), 101-114.

Nonetheless, Margaret Fell's pamphlet advanced the reform further, and in more sustained ways. Not only did she list additional examples of women's speaking and leadership ministries in the Old and New Testaments, but she also challenged directly flawed interpretations of Paul's teachings, elucidating their contextual concerns. Thus, while it cannot be said that Margaret Fell's most important essay was the first addressing of the subject, it does break new ground as the first contextual and historical-critical challenging of flawed interpretations of Paul's writings that had been hitherto uncontested, paving the way for modern critical and feminist biblical studies.[11]

In particular, two of Paul's statements were looked at more closely, as their primary target is not the female gender itself, but two contextual issues: the need to be well-versed in Jewish teachings, and the need to speak and act in upstanding ways, rather than gossiping or pratting irresponsibly.[12] These concerns would thus apply to men as well as women. Paul's restrictions, therefore, address not ontological matters of gender—literally—they reflect: (a) concerns over non-Jewish Jesus-adherents becoming biblically grounded before teaching others, and (b) the importance of speaking and acting with decorum rather than doing so in divisive ways. On the first issue (1 Corinthians 14:34-35, NRSV):

11 See Mary Anne, Schofield, "'Womens Speaking Justified': The Feminine Quaker Voice, 1662-1797," *Tulsa Studies in Women's Literature* 6.1 (1987): 61–77; Margaret Olofson Thickstun, "Writing the Spirit: Margaret Fell's Feminist Critique of Pauline Theology," *Journal of the American Academy of Religion* 63.2 (1995): 269–279.

12 For more extensive treatments of these biblical passages and Paul's inclusion of women in ministry roles, see Paul N. Anderson, *From Crisis to Christ: A Contextual Introduction to the New Testament* (Nashville: Abingdon, 2014), 254, 286-288.

> Women should be silent in the churches. For they are not permitted to speak but should be subordinate, as the law also says. If there is something they want to learn, let them ask their husbands at home. For it is shameful for a woman to speak in church.

Given the likelihood that Paul was meeting with men in the marketplace and teaching them Torah and biblical content—providing a worldview that countered the Corinthian pagan worship of Apollo, Aphrodite, Asclepius, and Roman gods—he was preparing new believers for worship in local synagogues on Sabbath and in house-churches on First Day. Thus, the reason women should keep silent and ask their husbands at home was not a matter of gender-capacity; it was a matter of getting caught up on the study of Jewish Scripture and who Jesus was theologically. This would especially have been a concern if some Corinthian women were already civic leaders, likely with societal influence, but who had not yet received formative instruction in matters of Jewish faith and practice that was the basis for Paul's teaching about Jesus as the Jewish Messiah/Christ.

On the second issue, 1 Timothy 2:11-12 is informed by the larger context, where Paul says, "Let a woman learn in silence with full submission. I do not permit a woman to teach or to have authority over a man; she is to keep silent." The problem in this situation is related to some particular women (especially younger ones, or widows) who were speaking and socializing in unbecoming (and perhaps seductive) ways (1 Tim 5:13-14):

> Besides that, they learn to be idle, gadding about from house to house, and they are not merely idle but also gossips

> and busybodies, saying what they should not say. So I would have younger widows marry, bear children, and manage their households, so as to give the adversary no occasion to revile us.

This relates to a further issue addressed in 1 Corinthians 11:5-16, where Paul declares that a woman prophesying or praying without her head covered is contentious. The issue there is Jewish modesty, but note that Paul also assumes that women were already prophesying and praying publicly, which he does not forbid. Thus, his counsel was not against women's public speaking or ministry; Paul's concern was modesty of dress and appearance while doing so. Given the fact that over a dozen pagan temples have been discovered in Corinth, and that cultic prostitution was a vibrant industry in this international metropolis, Paul's concern was for Jewish standards of dress and behaviors to be embraced among new believers, conforming to respectable customs.

Finally, when Paul advises that elders and pastors should be husbands of one wife (1 Tim 3:2; Titus 1:6), the issue is not a requirement that the minister be male and married (or not having been remarried if widowed or divorced). The concern was establishing a Jewish monogamous family model of leadership rather than polygamous alternatives. Note that here and elsewhere, Paul advocates for faithfulness to Jewish standards of faith and practice over and against wealth, societal status, and ability. Indeed, the moral actions and examples of leaders inevitably influence the ethos and standards of any organization or community. It cannot be otherwise.

In addressing these and other issues, Margaret Fell's prison-pamphlet on women's speaking justified *by* Scripture offers the first full challenge to the forbidding of women's public ministries in English language. In so doing, she points out that men *and* women are created in the Divine Image, that Israel *and* the Church are described in female terms biblically, that Jesus embraced women in his ministry, that the Holy Spirit was poured out on men *and* women at Pentecost, that women ministered *alongside* Paul in ways apostolic according to his writings, and that God used women's speaking *powerfully* in the Hebrew and Christian Scriptures alike.

Quakers, Women, and Public Ministry

Thus, the contribution of Margaret Fell and early Quakers on women's issues extended far beyond the Quaker movement, numbering around half a million adherents today. Rather, as Quaker women conducted organizational and outreach work together, they furthered ministry and service ventures extensively. Quaker women were also numbered among traveling ministers, and no fewer than a dozen women are numbered among the Valiant Sixty. These early Quaker leaders set out to evangelize the world in the first decade of the movement, following George Fox's three-hour sermon on Firbank Fell in 1652.[13] Elizabeth Hooton was one of the first followers of George Fox, Mary Fisher traveled to Adrianople to testify to the Sultan of Turkey, and Mary Dyer was hanged on Boston Commons—along with three other martyrs—for proclaiming the news that Christ is come to teach his people himself.

Other Quaker women of note include the Bible-teaching ministry of Deborah Darby, the prison-reform contributions of Elizabeth Fry, the abolitionist work of Lucretia Mott, Laura Haviland, and the Sisters Grimké, the women's rights advances of Susan B. Anthony

---

13 Elfrida Vipont numbers the Valiant Sixty at 66, *George Fox and the Valiant Sixty* (London: Hamish Hamilton, 1975), 128-129.

and Alice Paul, and such women authors as Hannah Whithall Smith and Jessamynn West.[14] For these and other good reasons, Margaret Hope Bacon rightly names Quaker women as "Mothers of Feminism," and much of that witness is due to the contribution of Margaret Fell, both in her written work and her compelling example.

While some well-meaning Christians continue to restrict women from committees of elders and public ministries based on narrow readings of biblical texts, Margaret Fell points the way forward with more adequate and accurate readings of women's speaking justified by Scripture, not against it. And, just as this message was world changing back in 1667, so it is needed among Bible readers today, as her witness—now in Modern English—indeed deserves a fresh hearing!

14 For a gathering of some two-dozen early Quaker women's writings, including other essays by Margaret Fell, see *Hidden in Plain Sight: Quaker Women's Writings, 1650-1700,* eds. Mary Garman, Judith Applegate, Margaret Benefiel, Dortha Meredith (Wallingford, PA: Pendle Hill Press, 1995).

Margaret Fell's "Women's Speaking Justified" in Modern English[15]

Translated and Annotated by Paul N. Anderson[16]

THE TEXT

Whereas women's speaking in churches has been objected to by many—including clergy, ministers, and others—condemning them for "meddling in the things of God" (based on 1 Cor 14:34-35 and 1 Tim 2:11-12), they are wrong in misunderstanding the Apostle's intentions. We shall thus clarify Paul's intentions in due course. First, however, let me lay down how God himself has manifested his mind concerning women, and also his will *for* women.

---

15 Written in Lancaster Castle Prison in 1666 and then finalized in 1667, when Margaret Fell, "the Mother of Quakerism," was imprisoned by the English government for holding worship in her home, Swarthmoor Hall, in Ulverston, England. The original title was "*Women's Speaking Justified, Proved, and Allowed of by the* Scriptures, *All such as speak by the Spirit and Power of the Lord Jesus. And how* Women *were the first that Preached the Tidings of the Resurrection of* Jesus, *and were sent by Christ's own Command, before he Ascended to the Father,* John 20:17," paraphrased here and translated into Modern English (using the NRSV) by Paul N. Anderson, 2026. In some cases, I have cited the full biblical reference alluded to by the author as a contextual service.

16 Paul N. Anderson serves as Professor of Biblical and Quaker Studies at George Fox University in Newberg, Oregon, and as Extraordinary Professor of Religion at the North-West University of Potchefstroom, South Africa.

Men And Women,
Created in the Divine Image

In the beginning (Gen 1:27-28),

> God created humans in his image, in the image of God he created them; male and female he created them. God blessed them, and God said to them, "Be fruitful and multiply and fill the earth and subdue it and have dominion over the fish of the sea and over the birds of the air and over every living thing that moves upon the earth."

Here God joins women and men together, in his own Image, making no distinctions between them, as humans do. For though humans be weak, they are also strong; and as the Lord said to the Apostle (2 Cor 12:9), "My grace is sufficient for you, for power is made perfect in weakness." And further (1 Cor 1:27-29),

> God chose what is foolish in the world to shame the wise; God chose what is weak in the world to shame the strong; God chose what is low and despised in the world, things that are not, to abolish things that are, so that no one might boast in the presence of God.

Thus, God sees no difference between the male and female, as some humans might, although the Serpent—that deceptive beast of the field—tempted the Woman[17] with a lie, subtly thinking of her as "the weaker vessel" (1 Pet 3:7) more inclined to listen when he said (Gen 3:5): "when you eat of it your eyes will be opened."

17 I here capitalize "the Woman," "the Man," "the Serpent," and "the Seed" etc. as typological references to humans, the tempter, and the work of Christ or the tempter within.

When the Woman saw that the fruit was good and able to make one wise, she was tempted, ate, and gave it to her husband to eat (v. 6). As a result, they both fell into temptation, leading to transgression and disobedience. Therefore, God said to Adam (who hid when he heard God's voice): "Have you eaten from the tree of which I commanded you not to eat?" And (speaking of weakness), the Man replied, "The woman whom you gave to be with me, she gave me fruit from the tree, and I ate." Then the Lord God said to the Woman, "What is this that you have done?" The Woman replied, "The serpent tricked me, and I ate" (vv. 12-14). On that point, the Woman was correct. Therefore, the Lord pronounced sentence upon the Serpent (v. 15):

> "I will put enmity between you and the
> woman and between your offspring and
> hers;
> he will strike your head, and you will
> strike his heel."[18]

So, let this Word of the Lord, which was from the beginning, stop the mouths of all who oppose women's speaking in the Power of the Lord; for he has indeed put enmity between the Woman and the Serpent.[19] And, if the Seed of the Woman does not speak, the Seed of the Serpent does speak; for God has put enmity between the two Seeds. Thus, those that speak against the Woman and her children speaking, speak out of the

---

18 This passage is also seen as a prophecy as to the power of Christ's victory over the Powers in his death and resurrection (Mark 13:25; John 12:31; Eph 6:12; 1 Pet 3:22; 1 John 3:8; Rev 20:10).

19 Note the reference to Christ, the pre-existent Word (John 1:1-5).

envy of the old Serpent's Seed. For God has fulfilled his Word and his Promise (Gal 4:4-7):[20]

> But when the fullness of time had come, God sent his Son, born of a woman, born under the law, in order to redeem those who were under the law, so that we might receive adoption as children. And because you are children, God has sent the Spirit of his Son into our hearts, crying, "Abba! Father!" So, you are no longer a slave but a child, and if a child then also an heir through God.

Israel and the Church Described as Women

Moreover, the Lord is pleased, when he mentions Israel, to call her *by the name of a woman*, by his prophets, saying (Isa 54:6), "For the Lord has called you like a wife ... like the wife of a man's youth."[21] Further, "How long will you waver, O faithless daughter? For the Lord has created a new thing on the earth: a woman encompasses a man" (Jer 31:32). And David, when he was speaking of Christ and his Church, describes the glories of the king's daughter, dressed in gold, who evokes gladness and rejoicing upon entering the king's palace (Isa 45:7-14). Likewise, when King Solomon speaks of Christ and his Church, calls her "the fairest among women" (Songs 1:8; 5:9).[22] Further, John, when viewing the wonder in Heaven, saw a woman clothed with the sun, with

20 Fell lists Gal 4:4-5, but vv. 6-7 also fill out the fuller meaning of the passage.

21 Fell uses the word "Church" here.

22 A spiritualized interpretation, there.

the moon under her feet, and a crown of twelve stars on her head (Rev 12:1-2).

Thus, in biblical perspective, both Israel and the Church of Christ are presented as a *woman*, and those that speak against *this* woman's speaking, speak against the Church of Christ, and the Seed of the Woman, whose Seed is Christ. In other words, those that speak against the Power of the Lord and the Spirit of the Lord speaking through a woman—simply because of her sex as a woman, not regarding the Seed, Spirit, and Power that speaks through her—such *speak against Christ and his Church*. They are of the Seed of the Serpent, wherein enmity resides. As God the Father saw no male-female difference in the first Creation, nor ever since, he has always shown regard for the weak out of his mercy and loving-kindness. So also his Son, Christ Jesus, confirms the same thing when the Pharisees asked him if it were lawful for a man to put away his wife. He answered and said unto them (Matt 19:4-6):[23]

> Have you not read that the one who made them at the beginning "made them male and female," and said, "For this reason a man shall leave his father and mother and be joined to his wife, and the two shall become one flesh"? So they are no longer two but one flesh. Therefore what God has joined together, let no one separate.

Again, Christ Jesus, when he came to the city of Samaria and Jacob's well, was pleased to preach the Everlasting Gospel to the woman at the well, who said to him: "'I know that Messiah is coming' (who is called Christ). 'When he comes, he will proclaim all things to

23 Jesus here defends the full dignity of the wife as a full partner in marriage, not a commodity to be dismissed or ignored.

us.' Jesus said to her, 'I am he, the one who is speaking to you'" (John 4:25-26). And he also said to Martha, when she declared her belief that her brother would rise again on the last day: "I am the resurrection and the life. Those who believe in me, even though they die, will live, and everyone who lives and believes in me will never die. Do you believe this?" (11:25-26). And then Martha—a woman—made a powerful confession (v. 27): "Yes, Lord, I believe that you are the Messiah, the Son of God, the one coming into the world."[24]

Jesus and Women in the Gospels

Remember also that Woman, who came unto Jesus with an alabaster jar of precious ointment and poured it on his head as he sat at table. Clearly this Woman knew more of the secret Power and Wisdom of God than his disciples did, who were filled with indignation against her. Yet Jesus declared: "Let her alone; why do you trouble her? She has performed a good service for me.... Truly I tell you, wherever the good news is proclaimed in the whole world, what she has done will be told in remembrance of her" (Mark 14:6-9). And further, Luke presents the scene in this way (Luke 7:44-50):

> Then turning toward the woman, he said to Simon, "Do you see this woman? I entered your house; you gave me no water for my feet, but she has bathed my feet with her tears and dried them with her hair. You gave me no kiss, but from the time I came in she has not stopped kissing my feet. You did not anoint my head with oil, but she has anointed my feet with

24 Adding to Fell's work, note that the Samaritan woman, Martha, and Mary Magdalene all make apostolic confessions in the Gospel of John.

> ointment. Therefore, I tell you, her many sins have been forgiven; hence she has shown great love. But the one to whom little is forgiven loves little. Then he said to her, "Your sins are forgiven." But those who were at the table with him began to say among themselves, "Who is this who even forgives sins?" But he said to the woman, "Your faith has saved you; go in peace."

Following this scene, Luke 8:1-3 presents women who are supporting Jesus and his ministry, financially and personally, out of their own resources. These include Mary Magdalene, Joanna (the wife of Herod's steward, Chuza), Susanna, and others.[25] At the Crucifixion, it is *women* who stood by Jesus, while the men were afar off (Matt 27:55-56; Mark 15:40-41); and women of Jerusalem wept for him. Jesus then addressed them, saying: "Daughters of Jerusalem, do not weep for me, but weep for yourselves and for your children" (Luke 23:28).

Thus we see that Jesus embraced the love and grace extended to him by women. He did not despise it, and according to Scripture, Jesus received as much love,

---

25 Fell places this reference following the women at the cross, but it follows more directly after Luke 7. Note that these women were persons of financial means and supporters of Jesus and his ministry. There is no biblical reference to Mary Magdalene being a woman of ill repute; that association was first advanced by Pope Gregory the Great in the 6th century CE—perhaps as a linking of the unnamed woman in Luke 7:36-50, followed by references to Mary Magdalene, Joana, and Susanna in 8:1-3—but connections Luke does *not* make. Likewise, the woman caught in adultery in John 8:1-11 is unnamed, so there is not even a hint that Mary Magdalene was a woman of questionable repute in the actual biblical texts; rather, the opposite is likely the case.

kindness, compassion, and tenderness from women as he did from others. And after his cruel treatment on the cross, it is Mary Magdalene, Mary the mother of James, and Salome, who brought spices to anoint him upon his burial (Mark 15:40). On the week's First Day, women came to the tomb at the rising of the sun, asking who will roll away the huge stone from the tomb's entrance (Mark 16:1-4; Luke 24:1-2). According to Matthew (28:2), an angel moved the stone aside in the midst of a great earthquake, and according to Luke 24:4-9,

> ...suddenly two men in dazzling clothes stood beside them. The women were terrified and bowed their faces to the ground, but the men said to them, "Why do you look for the living among the dead? He is not here but has risen. Remember how he told you, while he was still in Galilee, that the Son of Man must be handed over to the hands of sinners and be crucified and on the third day rise again." Then they remembered his words, and returning from the tomb they told all this to the eleven and to all the rest.

Thus, it was *women*—Mary Magdalene, Joanna, Mary the mother of James, and the other women—who told these things to the Apostles. Their words seemed like idle tales, and the Apostles did not believe them at first. However, to those of you who despise women and their so-called weakness, thinking yourselves to be so wise, Christ used those who were *weak in human eyes* to display his glory. It is to the *women* that he declared: "Greetings!" As they hugged his feet and worshiped him, he then commanded: "Do not be afraid; go and tell my brothers and sisters to go to Galilee; there they will see me" (Matt 28:9-10). And in John 20:16-18, the dialogue between weeping Mary Magdalene and

Jesus at the tomb leads to her becoming *the apostle to the Apostles*:[26]

> Jesus said to her, "Mary!" She turned and said to him in Hebrew, "*Rabbouni*!" (which means Teacher). Jesus said to her, "Do not touch me, because I have not yet ascended to the Father. But go to my brothers and say to them, 'I am ascending to my Father and your Father, to my God and your God.'" Mary Magdalene went and announced to the disciples, "I have seen the Lord," and she told them that he had said these things to her.

Apostolic and Ministering Women in the New Testament

So, for those of you who still despise the message of the Lord delivered by means of apostolic women, what would have happened to the redemption of all humanity if the Apostles had rejected their gospel message concerning the Resurrection, just because they happened to be women? And further, what if the women's tenderness and heartfelt love had not been activated by Christ's mercy, grace, and forgiveness they had received—which men also received—during his ministry? After all, it is not the men who beheld the Crucifixion up close, but from a distance, or who sat watching, waiting, and weeping at the tomb as witnesses to the Resurrection, but the *women* (Matt 27:55-56; Mark 15:40-41). And further, were it not for Mary Magdalene, who carried the news of the Resurrection

26 My language, there.

to the disciples, how else would they have known (John 20:18)?[27]

How blessed and glorious is the amazing Lord! For the bulk of humanity, claiming human wisdom without knowing God, is always ready to disparage the weak. But God has exposed human wisdom as foolishness (1 Cor 1:25): "For God's foolishness is wiser than human wisdom, and God's weakness is stronger than human strength."

For instance, in Acts 18:24-28, note how Aquilla and Priscilla (a *female* teacher!) tutored Apollos and instructed him more fully in the ways of God. He was already eloquent and mighty in his exposition of the Scriptures; yet he did not despise what Priscilla spoke to him, due to her being a woman, as many now do. Therefore, when we consider the Apostle's words in context, Paul's first concern in 1 Corinthians 14:34-35 is to exhort the Corinthians unto loving charity and unity, and to not speak in unknown tongues without an interpreter. Paul's goal is thus to further mature understanding, not senseless drivel. After all, the spirits of the prophets are always subject to the prophets' discernment, for God is not the author of confusion, but of peace (vv. 32-33).

Note, though, that women were *already speaking* in the Corinthian church when Paul instructed them to keep silence (vv. 6-12); for the purpose in sharing a song, a teaching, or a prophecy is to be understood meaningfully and in good order. That being the case, if there is confusion due to people speaking in unknown tongues, the important thing is to have an interpreter present. If an interpreter is not present, men also are commanded to keep silent, so that vocal ministry can be an ordered encouragement to all (vv. 26-32):

27 Mary Magdalene was the first person to behold the Resurrected Lord (John 20:11-17).

> What should be done then, my brothers and sisters? When you come together, each one has a hymn, a lesson, a revelation, a tongue, or an interpretation. Let all things be done for building up. If anyone speaks in a tongue, let there be only two or at most three and each in turn, and let one interpret. But if there is no one to interpret, let them be silent in church and speak to themselves and to God. Let two or three prophets speak, and let the others weigh what is said. If someone sitting receives a revelation, let the first person be silent. For you can all prophesy one by one, so that all may learn and all be encouraged ... as in all the churches of the saints.

This is why Paul calls for obedience to the orderly command of the Lord (v. 37), and the reason that Paul instructs women to ask their husbands at home is not a matter of gender preference (although remember how Eve was deceived in the Garden; 1 Tim 2:14); it is a matter of biblical instruction. The issue is the new believer's biblical knowledge, so that public ministry can be both grounded and edifying.[28] Yes, prophesying in tongues might be a sign for unbelievers, and Paul even

---

28 Most likely, Paul had been meeting with male Gentile believers in the marketplace for months, teaching them about the Jewish Scriptures and the Laws of Moses. Thus, the admonition to consult with husbands before sharing in public worship was designed to further the biblical foundation of their vocal ministry, to avoid confusion and uninformed teachings. It was not a matter of male superiority or female subordination; the issue was instructing Gentile believers in Jesus as the Jewish Messiah/Christ in the wisdom and ways of Jewish faith and practice.

quotes the Lord's words in Isaiah 28:11: "By people of strange tongues and by the lips of foreigners I will speak to this people, yet even then they will not listen to me" (1 Cor. 14:21). Further, Paul claims to speak in tongues more than any of the Corinthians, but it's better to utter five words of meaningful ministry than ten thousand words of confusing babble (vv. 19-20).

Problematic Demeanor, *Not* a Matter of Gender

So, how does all this relate to women's speaking in the church and the Power of the Everlasting Gospel that still needs to be preached? As we are reminded in Acts 2:16-21, the prophecy of Joel 2:28-32 is indeed fulfilled in that sons and daughters will indeed prophesy, and both young and old will see visions and dream dreams. Thus will the great and time-changing Day of the Lord be actualized, and all who call upon the name of the Lord will be saved. Therefore, Paul advises when visitors join their meetings, rather than speaking in tongues confusingly, let all people prophesy meaningfully (men *and* women) so that (1 Cor 14:24-25):

> ... an unbeliever or outsider who enters is reproved by all and called to account by all. After the secrets of the unbeliever's heart are disclosed, that person will bow down before God and worship, declaring, "God is really among you."

Paul thus did not say that women should not speak prophetically if the Spirit of God and revelation is poured out upon them; rather, those who are under strife, confusion, and malice should not be speaking in meetings for worship—in this case, particular women of Corinth—not women in general. Contextual issues are clarified further in 1 Corinthians 11:1-16, where

Paul calls for people to imitate him as he imitates Christ (v. 1). In this passage, women are clearly praying and prophesying, and Paul does not command them to stop. Rather, he calls them to do so in societal modesty—covering their heads—as a means of embracing Jewish traditions and not being confused in relation to ethical social norms. It would be likewise strange for a man to prophesy with his head covered, so Paul is appealing for cultural respectability here, given that men need women and women need men, in loving mutuality.

Returning again to 1 Timothy 2:8-14, Paul's central exhortation and concern that reverent prayer and supplication be made in all meetings for worship, involving the lifting up of holy hands without anger or dissention:

> I desire, then, that in every place the men should pray, lifting up holy hands without anger or argument, also that the women should dress themselves in moderate clothing with reverence and self-control, not with their hair braided or with gold, pearls, or expensive clothes, but with good works, as is proper for women who profess reverence for God. Let a woman learn in silence with full submission. I do not permit a woman to teach or to have authority over a man; she is to keep silent. For Adam was formed first, then Eve, and Adam was not deceived, but the Woman was deceived and became a transgressor.

Here the Apostle addresses directly the husband-wife relationship in terms of one being subject to the other, and one having authority over another, bringing in the story of Adam and Eve. However, that's a strained connection to make regarding who should be allowed to preach or speak in meetings for worship. Genesis 2-3 has no direct bearing on Christian worship in Corinth. Rather, the main concern of the Apostle is modesty of apparel—what to wear and what not to wear—and thus sobriety versus shamefulness. If women's braided hair, jewelry of gold and pearls, or provocative clothing should diminish their husbands' authority in a public meeting for worship, they should embrace reverence and modesty, displaying godliness with good works. Their presence should bespeak dignity and sobriety, not ostentation or allurement.

And if the Power of the Holy Spirit—the Spirit of the Lord Jesus—be poured out upon them, empowering them with a message from the Lord, must they not speak the Word of the Lord unto the meeting? Just because some indecent and irreverent women might have caused Paul to call for modesty and sobriety in that particular context, this does not mean that Paul forbad women's speaking in all other ministry settings. On this score, recent interpreters of Paul—condemning and despising all vocal ministries of women, even in delivering the Message and Word of the Lord God—are just plain wrong. In Philippians 4:1-3, Paul praises the public ministries of women as yokefellows, laboring with him and others in the furthering of the gospel:

> Therefore, my brothers and sisters, whom I love and long for, my joy and crown, stand firm in the Lord in this way, my beloved. I urge Euodia and I urge Syntyche to be of the same mind in the Lord. Yes, and I ask you also, my loyal companion, help these women, for they have struggled beside me in the work of the gospel, together with Clement and the rest of my coworkers, whose names are in the book of life.

Likewise in Acts 1:14, the Apostles are joined together in prayer and supplication with women, as well as men: "All these were constantly devoting themselves to prayer, together with certain women, including Mary the mother of Jesus, as well as his brothers." So, where would the mission of the Apostles been if they had not allowed women to participate in union and fellowship with the Spirit of God wherever it was revealed? Thus, all this opposition and denial of women's speaking in worship has arisen from the bottomless pit—the spirit of darkness—that has arisen over hundreds of years during the Night of Apostasy, in which God's revelations have been overlooked. That darkness has thus forbidden truth to be spoken, by both men and women, lest it be approved by the bond and compass of that darkness.

The misery of past ages thus continues to this day, as it did under the reign of the Beast, which John envisioned, rising out of the sea and out of the earth, having seven heads and ten horns, in Revelation 12-17. In this great city of Babylon, the Woman sitting on the scarlet-colored Beast persecuted the saints (17:4-6):

> The woman was clothed in purple and scarlet and adorned with gold and jewels and pearls, holding in her hand a golden cup full of abominations and the impurities of her prostitution, and on her forehead was written a name, a mystery: "Babylon the great, mother of whores and of earth's abominations." And I saw that the woman was drunk with the blood of the saints and the blood of the witnesses to Jesus.

And, this Woman has usurped authority for hundreds of years—attested by the murdering of the martyrs over past times and ages—killing those who would not join up with the evil empire.[29] Thus, the Spirit of Truth and the Power of the Lord Jesus Christ has largely been lost among those who have done this. The "mother of harlots" has sat as a queen and has given power unto the Beast to reign and make war with the saints of God for forty-two months, to overcome them (Rev 13:5). And, all the earth has worshiped him—those whose names are not written in the Lamb's Book of Life—slain from the foundation of the world (13:8; 17:8).

However, blessed be the Lord, whose time is now—redeeming the twelve hundred years of darkness and the Night of Apostasy, which is now come to an end—as the True Light now shines (Rev 22:16): "It is I, Jesus, who sent my angel to you with this testimony for the churches. I am the root and the descendant of David, the bright morning star." And, the true Church as the Bride of Christ is bidden come (v. 17), preparing herself for her husband, adorned in white linen, bright and pure (19:6-8), reported by John in this vision (21:10-11):

> And in the spirit he carried me away to a great, high mountain and showed me the holy city Jerusalem coming down out of heaven from God. It has the glory of God and a radiance like a very rare jewel, like jasper, clear as crystal.

And this (the true Church) is that Free-Woman, from which all the Children of the Promise are born—not the Children of the Bond-Woman Hagar, which engenders strife and bondage—but this is the *Jerusalem* that is free, which is the Mother of us all.

---

29 Language that describes the "Spirit of Darkness" and the imperial hegemony of Rome, among the Apostles, continued on in the era of Christendom from the reign of Constantine (who became a Christian in 312 CE) on. The Roman Empire became Christian in 380 CE under Theodosius.

And so, this Bond-Woman and her Children, which are born after the Flesh, have persecuted them that are born of the Spirit, even until now. But now, the Bond-Woman and her Seed are to be cast out, having imprisoned humanity so long in bondage and in slavery. This Bond-Woman and her Brood are to be cast out, and our Holy City, the *New Jerusalem*, is coming down from Heaven. For her light will shine throughout the whole earth, even as a jasper-stone, clear as crystal, which brings freedom, and liberty, and perfect redemption to her whole Seed. And this is that Woman and Image of the Eternal God, which God has owned, and does own, and will own for evermore.

Ministering Women in the Old and New Testaments

More might be added to this vision of biblical purpose, both from the Old and New Testaments, where it is evident that God made no difference of status between Man and Woman, but gave his good Spirit, as it pleased him, to both, as evidenced in the lives of Deborah, Huldah, and Sarah. For the Lord calls us all into service by his Prophet Isaiah (51:1-3):

> Listen to me, you who pursue
> righteousness, you who seek the LORD.
> Look to the rock from which you were
> hewn and to the quarry from which you
> were dug.
> Look to Abraham your father and to
> Sarah, who bore you,
> for he was but one when I called him, but
> I blessed him and made him many.
> For the LORD will comfort Zion; he will
> comfort all her waste places

> and will make her wilderness like Eden,
> her desert like the garden of the LORD;
> joy and gladness will be found in her,
> thanksgiving and the voice of song.

Further, Anna the prophetess, who was eighty-four years of age, served God with fasting and praying night and day in the temple. She encountered the Christ-child the very instant she entered the Temple. When old Simeon took baby Jesus in his arms, she gave thanks to the Lord and spoke to him of all who looked for the redemption of Jerusalem (Luke 2:36-38):

> There was also a prophet, Anna the daughter of Phanuel, of the tribe of Asher. She was of a great age, having lived with her husband seven years after her marriage, then as a widow to the age of eighty-four. She never left the temple but worshiped there with fasting and prayer night and day. At that moment she came and began to praise God and to speak about the child to all who were looking for the redemption of Jerusalem

And Philip the Evangelist, who was one of the seven deacons (Acts 6:5), into whose house the Apostle Paul entered on his travels, had four virgin daughters that did prophesy (21:8-9):[30]

---

30 Some scholars question whether the Philip mentioned in Acts 1, 6, and 8 is the same one living later on the coast in Acts 21. I find no basis for this distinction. Just as Philip is the one to whom Greek visitors to Jerusalem came seeking Jesus (John 12:21-22), he likely was a Hellenistic Jew, who later became a leader in Hierapolis in Asia Minor, according to Eusebius (*Church History* 3.31). In that setting, two of his ministering daughters are remembered as being with him until he died.

> The next day we left and came to Caesarea, and we went into the house of Philip the evangelist, one of the seven, and stayed with him. He had four unmarried daughters who had the gift of prophecy.

Therefore, let this serve to stop those opposing the Spirit and limiting the Power and Spirit of the Lord Jesus, whose Spirit is poured out upon all flesh—both Sons *and* Daughters—now in his resurrection ministry. For since the time that the Lord God created humans in his own Image, he made them Male *and* Female. And, since Christ Jesus, as the Apostle says, was born *of* a woman—overshadowed by the Power of the Holy Ghost—her holy offspring was called the Son of God. Further, when he manifested his love, will, and mind upon the earth, he did so to the woman of Samaria, to Martha, to Mary her sister, and to several others, as shown above. Finally, after his Resurrection, Jesus manifested himself unto women first, even before he ascended unto his Father, especially Mary Magdalene on the First Day of the Week (Mark 16:9; John 20:14-18).

Thus, the Lord Jesus has manifested himself and his Power to all—without respect of persons or their genders—so let all mouths be stopped that would limit him whose Power and Spirit are infinite, and who is outpouring it upon all flesh. So, in answer to these two Scriptures that have been such a stumbling-block, and of which the Ministers of Darkness have made such a mountain, the Lord is removing all this, and taking it out of the way.

M. F.[31]

---

31 This was the original conclusion of Margaret Fell's essay in 1666; later she added a postscript, expanding upon some of her earlier arguments.

Postscript:[32]

As an addition to the above essay, I offer here a further expansion upon Paul's directives that women should be silent in the church and subservient to their husbands. First, needing to be clarified contextually, "Women should remain silent in the churches. They are not allowed to speak, but must be in submission, as the law says" (1 Cor 14:34). And second, "A woman should learn in quietness and full submission" (1 Tim 2:11).

Clarifying What Paul's Writings Do and Do *Not* Say

Obviously, if these passages apply to all women, then those who are widows, or single, are excluded from Paul's injunctions. They have no husbands to learn from, so subservience is irrelevant. Further, Philip had four unmarried daughters that were prophetesses, whose spoken ministries the Apostle did *not* forbid. Thus, if the above verses were to apply to *all* women, Paul would have contradicted himself.[33] Rather, Paul's taking issue with younger widows going from house to house as idlers and busybodies has to do with their be-

---

32 Margaret Fell added this postscript in 1667.

33 Note that Paul extends greetings to ministering women leaders in Romans 16: Phoebe, a deacon of the church in Cenchreae (v. 1); Priscilla, a co-worker in Christ Jesus (v. 3); Mary, a worker (v. 6); Junia, outstanding among the Apostles (v. 7); and Tryphena, Tryphosa, and Persis—women who work hard in the Lord (v. 12). Other women are also greeted, as well; a full third of the two-dozen Christian leaders mentioned in Romans 16 are female. Thus, in addition to the women ministers referenced in Philippians 4:2, Paul clearly sees women as co-laborers with him and other Apostles in gospel ministry, so his particular directives are addressing contextual issues related to societal norms rather than gender-related limitations of women's public speaking in general.

havior, not their gender (1 Tim 5:11-15). And likewise, women *are* ministering in 1 Corinthians 11-14, so the concern is for them to do so respectably and fittingly.

As the Church is the Bride of Christ, the Bible is not against the female gender overall (Rev 19:7; 21:9). And indeed, as the prophecy of Joel 2 is fulfilled in Acts 2:18, the pouring forth of God's Spirit led to God's daughters prophesying as well as God's sons, though blind priests say to the contrary, forbidding holy women to speak in the churches.

Further, when Paul calls for women's submission according to the Law, women who are led by the Spirit of God are not under the Law (1 Cor. 14:34). For Christ's abiding in both the male and the female is one, and his Word is made manifest through both men and women. He is the End [and fulfillment] of the Law for righteousness unto all who believe (Rom 10:4), so there is a distinction between women who were under the Law before the coming of Christ and those who have received the Spirit of Prophecy later.

Women's Powerful Speaking in the Old and New Testaments Alike

For indeed, Huldah, Miriam, and Hannah were all prophetesses, and they were by no means forbidden to speak while under the Law. As 2 Kings 22:14-20 reminds us, it is Huldah who spoke to the priest and the king's ambassadors:

> So the priest Hilkiah, Ahikam, Achbor, Shaphan, and Asaiah went to the prophet Huldah the wife of Shallum son of Tikvah son of Harhas, keeper of the wardrobe; she resided in Jerusalem in the Second Quarter, where they consulted her. She declared to them, "Thus says the Lord,

> the God of Israel: Tell the man who sent you to me: 'Thus says the LORD: I will indeed bring disaster on this place and on its inhabitants—all the words of the book that the king of Judah has read. Because they have abandoned me and have made offerings to other gods, so that they have provoked me to anger with all the work of their hands, therefore my wrath will be kindled against this place, and it will not be quenched.' But as to the king of Judah who sent you to inquire of the LORD, thus shall you say to him: 'Thus says the LORD, the God of Israel: Regarding the words that you have heard, because your heart was penitent and you humbled yourself before the LORD, when you heard how I spoke against this place and against its inhabitants, that they should become a desolation and a curse, and because you have torn your clothes and wept before me, I also have heard you, says the LORD. Therefore, I will gather you to your ancestors, and you shall be gathered to your grave in peace; your eyes shall not see all the disaster that I will bring on this place.'"

Now let us see if any of you, blind priests, can speak after the spiritually empowered manner of Huldah the prophetess. Can you who are against women's speaking offer a better sermon than she? Isaiah embraced the prophetess in his day and did not forbid her speaking or prophesying (Isa 8:3),[34] and Joel prophesied that

34 Their child also bore a prophetic name: *Maher-Shalal-Hash-Baz* means "quick to the plunder, swift to the spoil," a reference to Israel's destruction and exile (Isa 8:1-3).

handmaidens of the Lord would prophesy in the future (Joel 2:18-19). Are they not women also? Consider this, those of you that are against women's speaking, how in Acts 2, the Spirit of the Lord was poured forth upon daughters as well as sons. And, in Luke 1:42-45, when Mary came to greet Elizabeth in the hill country of Judea, the baby within her womb leapt, and she was filled with the Holy Spirit, declaring in a loud voice:

> Blessed are you among women, and blessed is the child you will bear! But why am I so favored, that the mother of my LORD should come to me? As soon as the sound of your greeting reached my ears, the baby in my womb leaped for joy. Blessed is she who has believed that the LORD would fulfill his promises to her!

Further, following Elizabeth's prophecy, Mary declared in spoken ministry (vv. 46-55):

> "My soul glorifies the LORD and my spirit
> rejoices in God my Savior,
> for he has been mindful of the humble
> state of his servant.
> From now on all generations will call me
> blessed, for the Mighty One has done
> great things for me— holy is his name.
> His mercy extends to those who fear him,
> from generation to generation.
> He has performed mighty deeds with his
> arm; he has scattered those who are
> proud in their inmost thoughts.
> He has brought down rulers from their
> thrones but has lifted up the humble.
> He has filled the hungry with good things
> but has sent the rich away empty.

> He has helped his servant Israel,
> remembering to be merciful
> to Abraham and his descendants forever,
> just as he promised our ancestors.

Think of it! Here you honor Mary's *Magnificat*, featuring her words in your *Common Book of Prayer*, and yet you forbid women's speaking in ministry today. Clearly these two women spoke prophetically of Christ, and they also preached better than the blind priests of that age, and likewise better than those who make use of their words in public worship nowadays. Note also in Ruth 4, how because of her faithfulness to Naomi, God provided a son through her Kinsman-Redeemer Boaz, who became the ancestor of King David, and finally the Lord Jesus (vv. 13-22). Thus, the women blessed her in the gate of the city, declaring (vv. 11-12):

> We are witnesses. May the LORD make the woman who is coming into your home like Rachel and Leah, who together built up the family of Israel. May you have standing in Ephrathah and be famous in Bethlehem. Through the offspring the LORD gives you by this young woman, may your family be like that of Perez, whom Tamar bore to Judah.

See also in the Book of Samuel, how Hannah blessed the Lord with magnificent words upon the Lord's answering her prayer. Can any of you, blind Priests, that speak against women's speaking, preach as powerful a message as this woman did? And yet, by making use of holy Scripture, you make a trade of this and other women's words (1 Sam 2:1-10):

> My heart rejoices in the LORD; in
> the LORD my horn is lifted high.

My mouth boasts over my enemies, for I
delight in your deliverance.
There is no one holy like the LORD; there
is no one besides you; there is no
Rock like our God.
Do not keep talking so proudly or let your
mouth speak such arrogance,
for the LORD is a God who knows, and by
him deeds are weighed.
The bows of the warriors are broken, but
those who stumbled are armed with
strength.
Those who were full hire themselves
out for food, but those who were
hungry are hungry no more.
She who was barren has borne seven
children, but she who has had many
sons pines away.
The LORD brings death and makes alive;
he brings down to the grave and raises
up.
The LORD sends poverty and wealth; he
humbles and he exalts.
He raises the poor from the dust and lifts
the needy from the ash heap;
he seats them with princes and has them
inherit a throne of honor.
For the foundations of the earth are
the LORD's; on them he has set the
world.
He will guard the feet of his faithful
servants, but the wicked will be
silenced in the place of darkness.
It is not by strength that one prevails;
those who oppose the LORD will be
broken.

> The Most High will thunder from heaven;
> the LORD will judge the ends of the earth.
> He will give strength to his king and exalt the horn of his anointed.

And, did not the Queen of Sheba also speak when she came to Solomon and received the Law of God, which she then preached in her own kingdom? She indeed spoke further when she blessed the Lord God that loved Solomon and set him on the throne of Israel, and this was the language of the Queen of Sheba (1 Kings 10:6-9).[35]

> The report was true that I heard in my own land of your accomplishments and of your wisdom, but I did not believe the reports until I came and my own eyes saw it. Not even half had been told me; your wisdom and prosperity far surpass the report that I had heard.... Happy are these your servants who continually attend you and hear your wisdom! Blessed be the LORD your God, who has delighted in you and set you on the throne of Israel! Because the LORD loved Israel forever, he has made you king to execute justice and righteousness.

And see what glorious expressions Queen Esther used to comfort the people of God, which caused joy and gladness of heart among all the Jews of her day, who prayed and worshipped the Lord in all places.[36] Her life was placed in jeopardy as she

---

35 Quoting her language here, adding to Fell's reference.

36 Fell connects the ancient Israelites with the true Church of God.

stood bravely against the King's command for the Jews to be killed in Persia. She went and spoke to the King, in the wisdom and fear of the Lord, by which she saved the lives of God's People. Thus, righteous Mordecai did not forbid her speaking but declared unto her (Esther 4:13-14):

> Do not think that in the king's palace you will escape any more than all the other Jews. For if you keep silent at this time, relief and deliverance will rise for the Jews from another place, but you and your father's family will perish. Who knows? Perhaps you have come to royal dignity for just such a time as this.

We likewise read how Judith spoke, what noble acts she did, and how she spoke to the elders of Israel, calling them to be steadfast in faith through manifold troubles (Judith 8:24-27):

> Therefore, my brothers, let us set an example for our kindred, for their lives depend upon us, and the sanctuary—both the temple and the altar—rests upon us. In spite of everything, let us give thanks to the LORD our God, who is putting us to the test as he did our ancestors. Remember what he did with Abraham and how he tested Isaac and what happened to Jacob in Syrian Mesopotamia, while he was tending the sheep of Laban, his mother's brother. For he has not tried us with fire, as he did them, to search their hearts, nor has he taken vengeance on us, but the LORD scourges those who are close to him in order to admonish them.

And read also her prayer in Judith 9:2-14, and how Uzziah had commended her, saying (Judith 8:28-31):

> All that you have said was spoken out of a true heart, and there is no one who can deny your words. Today is not the first time your wisdom has been shown, but from the beginning of your life all the people have recognized your understanding, for your heart's disposition is right. But the people were so thirsty that they compelled us to do for them what we have promised and made us take an oath that we cannot break. Now since you are a God-fearing woman, pray for us, so that the LORD may send us rain to fill our cisterns. Then we will no longer feel faint from thirst.

Concluding Reflections on Women's Speaking Justified *By* Scripture

So, these elders of Israel *did not forbid* a woman's speaking, as you blind priests do; yet you will make a trade of women's words to bring in money. And, you take these biblical texts and preach sermons upon women's words in the Bible, while still crying out: "Women must not speak! Women must be silent!" Thus, you are far from the minds of the Israel's elders, who praised God for a woman's speaking. Isn't that ironic![37] And, in so doing, you yourselves are playing the role of tattling and unlearned women—*busybodies*—whom the Apostle for-

37 Fell's point, here; it is ironic, and even hypocritical, that those opposing women's speaking in ministry are doing exactly what Paul objects to. It is *they* that are the unlearned tattlers and busybodies, not women proclaiming biblically the gospel of Christ.

bids to speak, as they were transgressing the Law and its graces.[38]

Further, remember how it was the wise woman of Abel, who averted the destruction of an entire city by making a deal with Joab, offering up the head of the traitor Sheba in 2 Samuel 20. She thus declared (v. 19): "I am one of those who are peaceable and faithful in Israel; you seek to destroy a city that is a mother in Israel; why will you swallow up the heritage of the Lord?" As a result, Joab called off the siege, and his army departed in peace. In that instance, a woman's speaking averted a massacre.

So, yes, tattlers and busybodies are forbidden to preach in Paul's letter to Timothy, but in the true Church of Christ, sons and daughters *do* prophesy; women labor in service to the gospel; and the Church as the Bride of Christ learns from him, leading both women and men into liberating truth, through the workings of the Holy Spirit—the Spirit of Truth—accessible to male and female believers alike.[39] Thus, the question is not how believers might be taught by a woman or a man, but how they might be taught by the Spirit of Christ, which now leads us into truth if we will but attend and follow.[40]

And how about Philip's four prophesying daughters? As virgins, they had no married partners, but was not Christ their Husband, from whom to learn

---

38 This is the promise of John 14-16, that the Holy Spirit—the Spirit of Christ—is available to all believers, leading them into truth and giving them unction to be apostolic stewards of Christ's Word, if faithfully discerning and sharing it.

39 The goal of the believing hearer, thus, is not simply to listen to a human vessel. The goal is to attend and discern the divine Word coming through the faithful minister.

40 My digest of Fell's larger argument.

and discern? And if they indeed learned from Christ as their Husband, should not their speaking be listened to as the Word of Christ himself? Thus, in contrast to those Corinthian women who are ignorant of the Scriptures—not having been instructed in the ways of Jewish Scripture by Paul in the marketplace as their husbands were—those who preach that which they have received of the Lord God are serving the gospel well.[41]

However, those forbidding that women should speak in the church have their heads covered falsely—by the Pope, the head of the False Church (Rev 17)—which is against women's speaking in the True Church, which abides under the headship of Christ Jesus as his authentic Bride. Here, Christ is the Head of both male and female, who may speak; and the Church is called a Royal Priesthood of Believers according to 1 Peter 2:9.

Therefore, as the Spirit and the Bride of Christ, the True Church says to us all (Rev 22:17):

> "Come. And let everyone who is thirsty come. Let anyone who wishes take the water of life as a gift."

And, that includes women as well as men. Finally, note that when the chorus answers, saying "Amen!" (v. 20), that heavenly affirmation is given by both women as well as men, as both women and men are included in his Bride, the True Church. And in the end, Christ Jesus, who goes on conquering, slays with the Sword of his mouth, continues to speak through his Saints, which include women's speaking, as well as men's. Thus, the Lamb and the Saints shall have the victory: the true

41 My analysis of what was really going on in Corinth. See Paul N. Anderson, *From Crisis to Christ: A Contextual Introduction to the New Testament* (Nashville: Abingdon, 2014), 240-258, 276-292.

speakers of men and women over the false speakers of the world.

On Universal Ministry and Particular Vocations

Paul N. Anderson

If you are a Christian, you are a minister. The question is not *if* a follower of Jesus will minister; the question is *how*. As Elton Trueblood observed, the church of Jesus Christ is a ship that carries no passengers, for all are members of the crew. And, as Margaret Fell reminds us, the universal ministry of the Jesus movement includes women as well as men, young as well as old, and the simple as well as the learned.

Sometimes, however, we confuse Christian ministry in general with particular organizational programs. Christian ministry might involve serving within a designated role or position, but that need not be the case. Service and ministry are applications of divine love: first, identifying a human need, and then addressing that need, energized and empowered by the love of Jesus Christ. As John Woolman puts it in his *Journal* (1720-1742),

> The outward modes of worship are various, but wherever men [and women] are true ministers of Jesus Christ it is from the operation of his spirit upon their hearts, first purifying them and thus giving them a feeling sense of the conditions of others.

As we receive "a feeling sense of the conditions of others"—seeing others through the eyes of Christ, or seeing others as Jesus himself (Matt 25:31-46)—we cannot help but be moved with compassion to address human needs, both individually and structurally. Individually, there's never nothing that can be done to alleviate the suffering of others. We think globally but act locally. And structurally, sometimes societal and economic realities need to be addressed programmatically in order to make this a more just, prosperous, and peaceable world. Those advances may require long-term planning and institutional organization, but they always begin with a sensing of human need, moved by divine love.

Christian Ministry as a Calling to Love

At the heart of the teaching and example of Jesus is the calling to love. When challenged with a "trick question" as to which was the greatest of the Commandments, Jesus cites the *Shema* (Deut 6:4) as the first Commandment: the call to love the Lord God with all of our hearts, souls, minds, and strength. The vertical dimension of love fulfills the first four of the Commandments in Exodus 20, and the second Commandment fulfills the other six (citing Lev 19:18): command us to love one's neighbor as oneself (Mark 12:29-31). The cross of Jesus Christ is both vertical and horizontal, and we are called to meet at the center of the two.

Jesus, however, doesn't stop there; he also commands us to love our enemies. This is one of the most radical features of his teachings. The Gentiles might love those who love them, but to love our enemies—even those who hate us—sets a transformative example with world-changing possibilities (Matt 5:38-48; Luke 6:27-36). Turning the other cheek refuses to cower or to retaliate when threatened with a backhanded slap; going the extra mile goes beyond the minimal requirement, exercising love for occupying forces; handing over one's undergarments exposes harsh systems of crediting, when the wealthy might actually seek to conscript a debtor's property or land.[42] The third way of Jesus reminds us that there's always an alternative to violence, bribery, or coercion. The Kingdom of Christ is one of truth, not violence (John 18:36-37), and the truth indeed sets us free (8:32).

In addition to loving God, neighbor, and enemy, Jesus calls us also to love one another; and sometimes, extending grace and love within community might be the most difficult exercise of all. In so doing, however, Jesus invites us into partnership as his loving *friends*—not subservient slaves—but missional partners with Christ, discerning his will and living responsively to his leadings (John 15:12-15):

> This is my commandment, that you love one another as I have loved you. No one has greater love than this, to lay down one's life for one's friends. You are my friends if you do what I command you. I do not call you servants any longer, because the servant does not know what the master is doing, but I have called you friends, because I have made known to you everything that I have heard from my Father.

Therefore, the invitation to follow Jesus involves embracing his callings to love—God, neighbor, enemies, and one another—accepting also his invitation to agency. In so doing, not only is Jesus furthering what he has heard from the Father, but we also are drawn into actualizing God's will on earth as it is in heaven

42 For more on this subject, see the work of Walter Wink: *Violence and Nonviolence in South Africa: Jesus' Third Way* (Philadelphia: New Society Publishers, 1987); and Paul N. Anderson, "Jesus and Peace," *The Church's Peace Witness*, Marlin Miller and Barbara Nelson Gingerich, eds. (Grand Rapids: Eerdmans, 1994), 105-130.

because we have attended, discerned, and minded what we have heard from the Living Lord.

On Particular Callings and the Priesthood of All Believers

While every believer is called to be a minister, particular roles in ministry are rightly designated and assigned within church communities and other organizations. In addressing the concerns of the early church, seven *deacons* were appointed to care for the needs of Gentile believers, who were being overlooked in the daily serving of food (Acts 6:1-6). As Paul and Barnabas traveled through southern Asia Minor on their first missionary journey, they appointed *elders* in every church—a Jewish system of corporate leadership—so that direction and decisions could be made in terms of community leadership (Acts 14:23). And, *overseers* as *pastors* were also chosen to shepherd flocks and to provide edifying instruction for the communities under their care (Acts 20:28).

As overseers, deacons, and elders are chosen in service to communities of worship, their lives should be exemplary and of upstanding character. Otherwise, the values of the community will be jeopardized (1 Tim 3:1-13; Titus 1:5-16). Paul also affirms the putting into play of spiritual giftedness, affirming such graces in public ministry as *apostles*, *prophets*, and *teachers* as the greater gifts (1 Cor 12:27-31). Those graces that serve the broader community are to be valued more highly, over and above those gifts, even if spectacular, that edify primarily the individual.

In Ephesians 4:11, pastors and teachers are referenced together as dual giftedness; these graces are mutually reinforcing. Rather than envying the giftedness of others, though, believers are reminded (1 Cor 12:4-7):

> Now there are varieties of gifts but the same Spirit, and there are varieties of services but the same LORD, and there are varieties of activities, but it is the same God who activates all of them in everyone. To each is given the manifestation of the Spirit for the common good.

Alongside his listing of spiritual gifts, Paul also includes the allegory of the Body of Christ as a vision of the church (Rom 12:3-8; 1 Cor 12:12-31; Eph 4:1-16). While different parts of the body have particular functions, they should both do their work well and should also do so in coordination with other parts. Complementarity is thus a factor of giftedness, not a matter of gender. Most important, though, is responsive connectedness to Christ the head of the Body—the Church—and that connectedness is central to being effective partners with Christ as his apostolic agents in the world.

Along these lines, when Jesus meets with his followers on First Day two millennia ago, as his first Post-Resurrection work, he comforts them saying "Peace be with you." Second, he commissions them as apostles: "As the Father has sent me, so I send you." Third, he breathes on them and declares: "Receive the Holy Spirit." Note that his commissioning is plural, not just an apostolic charge to a single individual. And the reason he commissions all believers as priestly apostles is that the hurting needs of the God-beloved world demand it: unless people's sins are forgiven, they are retained, and humanity languishes in graceless bondage (John 20:21-23).

This passage was central to Luther's doctrine of the priesthood of all believers, but it harkens back to the original intention of Jesus for the Church and the world. As Neave Brayshaw also reminds us, the Society of Friends "has rediscovered, neither easily nor quickly, the truth that it exists not for itself, but for the world's healing."[43]

On Callings Discerned and Recorded

In discerning a particular call to ministry, sometimes this relates to giftedness and the willingness to put God-given gifts into service. Along these lines, elders and other leaders within Christian communities should be ever at work in educating, exhorting, and encouraging emerging leaders in their gifts of ministry. In that sense, one of the greatest ministries a pastor or a Christian leader can offer is preparing members of one's flock for the ministries to which they have been called. The meeting is gathered for worship, and it is scattered for service. And after all, it is the sheep that bring forth the lambs, not the shepherd.

Paul reminds Timothy both to not neglect the gift that was his—received at the laying on of hands (1 Tim 4:14)—and also to rekindle it as needed (2 Tim 1:6). He also calls Timothy to do his best to present himself to God, "as one approved by him, a worker who has no need to be ashamed, rightly explaining the word of truth" (2 Tim 2:15). A calling to serve thus is a calling to prepare. Therefore, effectiveness in ministry involves both receptivity to the graces given by the Holy Spirit and responsibility in preparing for those functions and roles to which one has been called.

In discerning a particular call to ministry, this will often relate to one's experiences, both inwardly and outwardly. Inwardly, when noting the callings of the Hebrew Prophets (Moses, Isaiah, Jeremiah, Ezekiel) and Paul and John in the New Testament, several features accompany their calling narratives:

---

43 Neave Brayshaw, *The Quakers* (London: Friends Home Service, 1969), 348.

- First, some form of encounter with the Divine evokes a crisis: a burning-bush theophany, visions of angels in worship, hearing a divine voice, or encountering the Risen Lord on the road to Damascus or in worship.
- Second, humans are filled with a sense of awe and humbled inadequacy: a stammering tongue, unclean lips, too young or unprepared, falling to the ground as though dead.
- Third, God assures, redeems, and empowers the individual: Aaron will assist, an angel purifies his tongue with a burning coal, the Divine Voice provides encouragement and guidance.
- Fourth, the human is entrusted a sense of mission and a message: tell Pharaoh to let God's people go, keep proclaiming despite uneven receptions, God has created and gifted the prophet for the mission at hand, Ananias will support, a vision engenders hope.[44]

In discerning a calling from inward experience, becoming a steward of life's most transforming moments becomes a way forward, vocationally. Thus, embracing a calling is less a matter of actualizing all that one can be, and more a matter of giving all that one can give. As Paul declares, "Woe is me if I preach not the gospel" (1 Cor 9:16). In addition, discerning a calling sometimes emerges from outward awareness of what desperately needs to be done. Friends call this a "Concern"—a God-given conviction that particular human needs deserve to be addressed—leading to taking up a mantle

44 Paul N. Anderson, "Receiving Holy Callings, Becoming Wholly Responsive" (2 Parts) *Oikonomia Network* (February 2020): https://oikonomianetwork.org/2020/02/receiving-holy-callings-becoming-wholly-responsive/; (March 2020): https://oikonomianetwork.org/2020/03/receiving-holy-callings-becoming-wholly-responsive-part-ii/.

of service and leadership in the healing/redeeming of God's beloved world. Or, it might involve organizing a committee or a corporate means of addressing a set of human needs.

As the Apostle Paul describes his conviction that the divine word is as near as people's mouths and hearts, believing that salvation comes to those who believe inwardly and confess their faith outwardly, he delights in the belief that there is now no distinction between Jews and Gentiles. All can now be one in Christ (Rom 10:6-13). And yet, he feels moved with the Concern that there are not enough partners in the mission to get the work done. Thus, citing Isaiah 52:7, Paul continues in verses 14–15:

> But how are they to call on one in whom they have not believed? And how are they to believe in one of whom they have never heard? And how are they to hear without someone to proclaim him? And how are they to proclaim him unless they are sent? As it is written, "How beautiful are the feet of those who bring good news!"

Along these lines, a call to public ministry differs from the general calling to serve, entrusted to every believer. Particular callings—emerging either from inward vocation or outward concern—deserve to be acknowledged and supported by corporate meetings and church communities. Indeed, God ordains persons to particular ministries, but faithful communities must observe, acknowledge, and record a spiritual leader's giftedness for gospel ministry, which also implies the willingness to support them as needed. This support can be empowered by dedicating and assigning a man or woman unto a particular ministry, and yet, such a commissioning must be supported with prayer and counsel.

While a call to public ministry will normally be a lifelong vocation, particular venues of service—or chapters in one's life of ministry—will relate to particular charges and settings. Sometimes full-time or part-time ministry service is subsidized by a congregation or an organization. At other times, one's gainful occupation supports a ministry calling, and this was certainly the case for the Apostle Paul as a tent maker. Either way, the Christian minister's support should not be seen as a "paid service" as a contractual obligation; rather, it should be seen as being "released" for ministry, so that one's time and energies can be given fully to the charge one has been entrusted.

Embracing the Yoke of Christ

Within the universal ministry, including women as well as men, and the young as well as the mature, all followers of Jesus are exhorted to embrace his yoke. Whereas the yokes we fashion for ourselves chafe and fail to fit properly, his yoke fits us well and empowers the capacity to bear life's burdens with resilience and tenacity. As Jesus invites us in Matthew 11:28-30,

> Come to me, all you who are weary and are carrying heavy burdens, and I will give you rest. Take my yoke upon you, and learn from me, for I am gentle and humble in heart, and you will find rest for your souls. For my yoke is easy, and my burden is light.

Embracing the yoke of Christ first involves learning *about* Jesus, as his loving character is gentle and humble in heart. Therefore, with Thomas à Kempis, *The Imitation of Christ* becomes the calling of every believer: returning good for evil, embodying servanthood, embracing the outcast, healing the unclean, accepting the forsaken. This will involve a life of study, seeking to become like the object of our focus: Jesus.

In addition, though, to learning *about* Christ, we are also invited to learn *from* Christ, who teaches and guides faithfully by means of the work of the Holy Spirit, whom he and the Father will send to be with and in his followers (John 14:15-26; 15:26-27; 16:7-17). The Advocate, the Holy Spirit, the Spirit of Truth will remind believers of what Jesus has been teaching and will bring to present mindfulness the guidance and clarity needed for the given situation. Thus, the Holy Spirit *convinces* people of sin and righteousness and judgment, bringing unworldly peace and the fullness of joy.

Along these lines, preparation for Christian ministry is never a done deal, something that was wrapped up in a seminary course of study or an otherwise helpful educational program. Knowledge about can never replace intimate acquaintance with, and such is what Jesus came to bring as the heart of true Christian divinity (John 17:3): "And this is eternal life, that they may know you, the only true God, and Jesus Christ, whom you have sent."

In cultivating intimate acquaintance with Christ, daily Bible reading, prayer, and devotional practices are essential, and so are commitments to large- and small-group fellowship, ongoing study, and dedicated service.[45] If these sorts of disciplines are elements of the yoke of Christ—focused means of learning about and from the Living Lord within a dynamic Christocentricity—we find ourselves in something like

---

45 Along these lines, see Richard J. Foster, *Celebration of Discipline* (special edition, New York: HarperOne, 2018); and D. Elton Trueblood, *A Place to Stand: A Practical Guide to Christianity in Changing Times* (3rd edn. Newberg: Barclay Press, 2025).

a new religious order: what Elton Trueblood describes as the Order of Common Life.[46] And, this is the calling of every believer, which faithful Christian ministers are called to inspire. After all, on the ship of Jesus Christ, none of us are passengers; we are all members of the crew.

46 Paul N. Anderson, "A Dynamic Christocentricity—The Center of Faithful Praxis," *Quaker Religious Thought* 105 (2005): 20-36.

www.ingramcontent.com/pod-product-compliance
Ingram Content Group UK Ltd.
Pitfield, Milton Keynes, MK11 3LW, UK
UKHW040849300326
11567UKWH00008B/30

9 781594 982118

www.ingramcontent.com/pod-product-compliance
Ingram Content Group UK Ltd.
Pitfield, Milton Keynes, MK11 3LW, UK
UKHW040849300326
11567UKWH00008B/30

9 781594 982118